BETWEEN
HEAVEN AND EARTH

THE SOUL
PURPOSE

ALONE AT THE
CROSSROADS

Dear Jennifer!
Keep Smiling
Love Joy Mills
3/00

BETWEEN
HEAVEN AND EARTH

THE SOUL
PURPOSE

ALONE AT THE
CROSSROADS

BY
JOY MILLS, C.HT.

ibrary of Congress Number 99-093538
3BN 0-9671280-0-5

Published by Lightsource Publications

Cover photo by Benjamin Ealick

Book design by Steve Simmons

Printed by Gilliland Printing

First Edition: October 1998

Printed in the United States of America

To those who might judge me:

Thank you,

For without adversity,

I wouldn't have reached my full potential

and found my Way.

- J.M.

Contents

Acknowledgements

We need water.
The scent of water
in this
parched and arid time...

Unto the Heavens, our Universe
will guard and protect you
from all unwanted influence.
No evil will touch you,
for you are to bring peace to the earth.
Thankful for all the unseen, protective hands
that encompass you,
for Life is but an energy
that brings forth our gifts,
knowing we shall all prevail
when Life is through the door,
our Spirit awakens to
a brand new beginning.
So do not draw back from tomorrow,
embrace it.

This book was written for my own healing, and through it, I realized that thankfulness comes from inside the deepest facets of my human soul.

We all need to strive for a balance that can provide a continuum for moving, propelling us ever forward.

To my husband, Larry, for your silent, loving support. You know the deepest places in my heart, and have taught me the true meaning of a healthy relationship;

My beautiful children, forever reminding me of what Unconditional Love truly is;

The friends the Universe has allowed to walk the path with me, for all your love and support, never waning, even when I am so focused with the rigors of this busy time;

Pam, your wonderful, patient and kind spirit;

My management team, for all your belief and encouragement.

May each of you, named and unnamed, always have the true peace. My hope is that the Universe always guides and protects you.

There are two kinds of people in the world:
the Givers and the Takers.
The difference between the two is that
the Takers eat well,
and the Givers sleep well at night.

- - - - -

She had lived for years in the same manner: he'd been the dominant force in their relationship, powerful in both his stature, and his commanding presence. She'd been coasting along, aware only of the fact that he loved her. She was content to live through him, complacent in his shadow. Yet they had shared little in common, even from the very beginning.

The years had flown by, and with the passage of time, each began to discover new activities and began growing in different ways. Together, they had found a few mutual interests, yet somehow, through circumstances alone if by no other way, they seemed to be going in opposite directions.

But theirs had been a relationship that simply worked, which was rare nowadays. So she had drifted along, staying by him, because it was her duty, she told herself.

But it had become his duty to be her strength, she could realize only later -

But now things were changing. Although the few mutual interests in their life together remained the same, each could sense that something was different. It was as though the ever-quickening pace of the chaotic world outside had at last permeated their complacency, lending a sense of urgency in the house and within themselves as well. And while both knew that each still loved each other, they sensed a new beginning on the horizon resulting from a distinct sense of purpose to their own individual lives: their destinies were slowly taking shape and she began to realize that their predetermined paths were now leading them away from each other, and there was nothing that either could do about it. An unspoken sense of separation lingered between them, and the love that had initially brought them together was simply not the binding factor anymore.

Suddenly she realized that the path for each of them had always been different. Caught up in the day-to-day activities and influenced by his power, she had allowed herself to become lost in his oversoul because she was afraid to face her own. She had become the Taker, for she had unwittingly deprived herself of the opportunity to pursue her own purpose in life, just as he had been unwittingly cast as a Taker when she had become lost in his oversoul.

But it was only in finding and exerting her own positive energies that she began to realize the true purpose and meaning of her own existence. Fate had brought them together; their destinies would separate them, should each have the courage to follow their own individual paths. But she knew what had to be done, for while they could change their fate by staying together, they could not change their destinies.

She realized at last that the time would soon come for rebirth.

- - - - -

The Dead Sea and the Sea of Galilee are as old as Time itself. Both can teach us much about Life, not only from the historical and Biblical aspects, but through them, we learn about taking and giving as well.

The Dead Sea is the final destination for the Jordan river. As its name implies, it is a sterile body of water. Nothing flourishes there, for its waters contain an average of over 26 percent salt. And the shores are affected as well, for nothing grows: the soil around it is much too salty to sustain life. Hence, everything near and around it is affected by it. It simply sucks up the incoming water and remains stagnant.

Yet close by is the Sea of Galilee, through which the Jordan flows. Teeming with life both within and without, its banks provide an inviting oasis in the arid desert. Birds build their nests there, and children swim in its waters. And the Sea, ever dynamic, continually replenishes itself...

And so it has always been.

- - - - -

Every relationship or situation has the potential of turning us into Takers if we, figuratively speaking, eat well in the moment, but discount any feelings of lost self-empowerment or a loss of well-being we might experience as a result: Ultimately, we become fearful of facing our own oversoul.

When we begin to realize that we are discounting these feelings, we have experienced the first step in shedding the persona of a Taker: we have become aware that through our role as Takers, something of ourselves was lost.

This awareness commences when the totality of our mind-body-spirit is open and receptive. First, we experience what we might call the shadowy side: We are ready to "peek out into the sunlight." Where do we go from there?

Finding the answer becomes the search. It commences with the knowledge of where we began, and it allows to understand where we are in the Now, and continues when we contemplate where we would like to be in the future.

When this initially happens, we might look back over years past with regret. While it is beneficial to experience the regret to release the pain and other feelings which might accompany it, we must not allow ourselves to regret too long: If left unchecked, it is possible that the regret might turn into remorse, resulting in resentment of the other person, circumstances or situations with which we were involved. Unconsciously, we might build a wall of rage against the offending force, thereby blocking our abilities for self-help and self-fulfillment.

Sometimes, we are more afraid to challenge ourselves than we are to honestly face the other person or confront the situation at hand. But when the extraneous issues have been stripped away, we are left with nothing but ourselves.

Some of us may find that we have been channeling our energy into negativity and uncertainty, which inhibits any progress we might hope to make. Hence, we need to release the negativity and uncertainty by looking within ourselves, to our Higher Self. Such an experience allows a rebirth.[1]

But this experience takes time, for in many instances, changes simply do not happen overnight. We can take comfort in the fact, that although we may not presently be where we want to be, we can be where we were destined to be when we employ a combination of patience, faith and positive action. Over time, the journey becomes a series of winding roads.

Paradoxically, we might liken our initial birth to coming out from the sunlight into that darkened movie theater: we were whole and complete; we lacked for nothing. But once we arrived on the earth plane (and into the theater), we descended into consciousness: We were taught to think and conform to the standards of contemporary society, though we may have lost a part of ourselves in the process.

While most of these tenets are beneficial to not only society in general, but ourselves as well, some of them may have been self-defeating, especially if we were required to do what we thought we should be doing by discounting the voice of our own Higher power. Sometimes, this Voice is drowned out by the concept that we should feel guilty if we are happy, or that happiness comes from external circumstances, or that our identity is found only when we have someone special in our lives. Sometimes, our roles are choreographed to fit whatever has been considered "right" by society, or we may have been molded to fit the personal expectations or dreams of those individuals responsible for our upbringing.

Some of us may have wanted to take a different career path than what we actually chose, and then ended up miserable and wishing we'd heeded the advice from within. Some of us may have achieved all the material successes we could have ever hoped to attain and then some, yet still feel restless and unsettled inside. We might have found our ultimate happiness in the one we loved and cherished, only to find that circumstances and situations caused them to leave or fail us in some way. And some of us may have found our own inner peace, only to trash it later because we were taught that something always had to be wrong in our lives. Hence, we might feel as though we have experienced our life in a darkened movie theater.

Regardless of the circumstances, however, nothing ever happens solely by accident. We can be assured that being sequestered in that movie theater allowed us to experience life's shadowy side. We now need to step out of the shadows and "peek out into the sunlight:" The result, then, is a rebirth.

But to step out of the shadows, we have to cut ourselves loose from the tentacles of fear: we are required to step out with courage, faith and the belief that we will get what we need and realize that the Universe does indeed hold us accountable for our actions. We learn that we must pursue our own path, and that we must rely upon ourselves for happiness. We must realize that we were born alone, and that we will die alone. We learn that we already have everything we need within to make ourselves happy, and that in projecting our own positive energy out into the world, that positive things can, and will, return to us.

The rebirthing process itself is just as painful for the child as it is for the mother; as we commence in this process, we realize that we are both the child and mother, regardless of our gender. We become our own caretakers and supply ourselves with the values which will aid in our spiritual progression at this important time.

Life itself, then, becomes a continual cycle: gestation, fertilization, birth, death, decay, and finally, rebirth.

- - - - -

This book is based upon my experiences, years of work, and my teaching, all from the aspect of spirituality. It is about shedding who we were and the baggage that brought us to this point, facing who we are now, and creating the foundation to determine who we have yet to be. It was written, then, to assist you in your path toward your own spirituality and inner peace. We might be standing on a bridge we cannot cross and cannot burn, and for that reason we must remember to stay in the moment while keeping our goals in sight. Knowing what they are, we appreciate the process we must follow to get there.

This book does not, however, contain all the answers. If you feel that your issues are more of a psychological nature, rather than those of the spirit, my recommendation would be to seek out a qualified, competent therapist, for this book was not designed for use as a therapy tool.

As humans, we feel, and sometimes act upon our emotions, which limit can our spiritual growth and physical well-being. Yet when we allow ourselves to do so, we can begin a Higher level of learning and, by projecting our own positive energy, we can attract to us someone or something better than we ever could have imagined. We can begin to appreciate our world from a Higher perspective: that is, one fostered by a greater awareness, acceptance, understanding and a consistent inner peace.

Though we may experience remarkable spiritual growth, however, this does not mean that we cease to feel the emotions that we humans experience, for we are, after all, only human beings on this transitory earth plane, and Life can at times, deal us some heavy tragedies. But emotional states are transitory. When we are stuck in the moment, we can remind ourselves that it is the mind, and not the soul, that imposes the boundaries, and that it is the mind that will entrap us. But we can find our own path to close out the turmoil and stop the self-doubt, to discern the illusions from reality. We can learn to better define our responsibilities and arrest any backsliding which might imped our spiritual progress, and we can indeed rise above the destructive cycle of action and reaction.

And when we are able to access our own inner peace, we will have enough self-determination to cherish it, instead of trashing it.

It is a long, arduous path, but it is also one that is well worth the effort.

---

[1] It must be noted here that one is not advised by this author to attend rebirthing classes! Figuratively speaking, however, we rebirth ourselves when we begin to find ourselves.

- - - - -

My Warrior Nature reaches for
the deeper meaning,
no longer a split in my mind,
body or soul.
Focused, seeing my direction
as clear as a spring morning.
Look behind the face, in the eyes,
the window to the soul.

- - - - -

Four things to remember:

- - - - -

As we travel on our spiritual path, we need to remember four important principles, for they will enable us to see our goal more clearly:

1. *Complacency is dangerous;*
2. *We have been programmed to desensitize ourselves;*
3. *We tend to make the crossroads confusing; and*
4. *Enlightenment in its truest form is salvation.*

As we delve deeper into the significance of each of these principles, we appreciate their wisdom in defining our goals and possible pitfalls as we progress along our path. Although each is in some manner related to the other, they have their own individual value as well.

Not only is the number four significant to the principles above, but four reminds us of the natural forces which influence us: there are four main compass directions, four seasons in a year. Similarly, four natural elements will guide us and serve us well on our journey, embodied in Earth, Wind, Fire and Water.

As we are aware, the starting point is the self, and when we begin with ourselves, we will find that our most profound resource is inner peace.

We begin the path by contemplating the significance in strength and will, courage and fortitude, for these basic elements, when fully applied, will greatly assist us throughout our journey.

PART I

EARTH:
THAT WHICH GROUNDS US

*Complacency
is Dangerous*

The Higher Self will unite only when we have begun
to let go of all the old conditions,
no longer desperate to make it fit.
Finally, it comes together with ease.
Knowing that I can achieve a peaceful place that's not of external
people or things,
it hides inside the depths of my soul, the essence of who I am,
knowing the Plan
like knowing your name.
It's simple, but so complex
no place to analyze,
for you'll be assured of nothing
with pride and ego as your guides.

Rise above these things
that fester like a cold sore with no hope to heal.
Let go of your conditioned self,
for the seventh and eighth sense is only a
longing for most,
because this place frightens us
with no crisis looking for an elusive place that already exists.
I see a Higher, Divine Life without remorse, not regret,
for I am a willing participant in my own Destiny.

Somewhere, we were taught to create our fate
and then life is futile, for we are set adrift
in a world of our creation gone wild,
fighting as if we are challenged
but that's a challenge of our mind, not the Spirit,
where the answers are the purity lies awakened only
by wanting to change,
a redirecting our split course to a road designed
with no blocks,
only obstacles to learn, grow and free ourself.
No more chained to an awful place, but flying freely, giving and
receiving
all the Universe and Spirit has to offer.

Strength and will:
Passive and active

If we are allowed only one word each to define the terms strength and will, we might select the word power for strength, and determination for will. As we might initially believe, strength requires action, and will requires inaction.

Upon closer examination, however, we see that strength is in fact passive, whereas will is active, when they are applied internally. Strength, or power is generated when we are passive, quiet and have assumed a listening attitude. Will requires an active determination, for through the action of will we find our peace in the knowledge of strength.

It is easy to see only what we think we see, and not something else that might be on a different level!

- - - - -

Courage is not
Fortitude

Courage and fortitude are related, yet they are not the same.

Courage is defined as the ability to follow through with a plan of action; it is the ability to stand on our own feet, in spite of ourselves. This is the strength of the mind or body and will in the face of the danger or challenge before us.

Fortitude, however, is perpetuated by courage: when we possess courage, attributes of strength and will are already integrated within us. Now, we need the staying power to carry through, for at this point, we are already aware of the lessons we've learned.

We see, then, that one enhances the other.

Things left undone that are later completed, are a result of fortitude. We might have courage, but it is the energy of fortitude that motivates us toward completion of the task before us.

We need courage to stand on our own feet, then, in spite of ourselves. This, then, is the essence of our complex nature!

- - - - -

She was sitting on a cold grey stone in the mountains, over-

4

looking the brown hills and green valleys below. She felt the power in the very air there; it made her feel invincible. Nothing would stop her from finding and keeping her heart's desire.

You don't belong here.

Did she just hear those words?

She saw him standing alone, this strong Native American spirit. His power was almost overwhelming; he seemed unattainable. The word, 'trophy,' flashed through her mind.

You would have him only as a trophy.

She heard that voice again.

He was handsome, tall, blonde. A Blond Native American.

Pale eyes. Cold and sad. Eyes, that, even when focused upon her, seemed unfocused, gazing through her, rather than upon her. They reflected the pain in his soul that she could neither heal nor soothe. She could not comfort him. . .

She heard the mourning yells of the Natives; with her own power, she was holding him back. His spirit was dying.

- - - - -

She awoke with a start. Had she been dreaming?

- - - - -

I have been feeling so empty lately, he said to their wise, compassionate friend who was both a skilled counselor and listener. My friends are wonderful and we do a lot together. I have a good job, and it pays well. But I don't have any other training, and I don't want to do this type of work for the rest of my life.

Nothing makes sense in my world anymore. I don't know what I'm supposed to be doing with my life. I've felt this emptiness for the past year. . .

- - - - -

The One Voice Within

When we are clear and open, we know we can trust our inner selves and have the ability to listen to the small Voice within, the one that would never advise us to harm ourselves or somebody else.

Sometimes, when we are plagued by conflict, stray thoughts run rampant through our head, suggesting or advising us that we think or act in ways that are harmful to ourselves or others, that we are in some way justified to have the harmful thoughts or intentions they suggest, that they will serve us well, and that we should adopt negativity as our reality. Obviously, these voices are simply the manifestations of our own ego, created from the conflicts within and around us; sometimes, however, they are the results of the rampant extraneous energies from the outside world. (Since we humans can be highly telepathic, it is possible that we can pick up somebody else's negative thoughts!)

Nevertheless, when this happens, we can quiet the resulting chatter within by journaling our thoughts and through meditation, enabling the one clear, positive Voice to become louder. This Voice is the one that would never suggest that we harm ourselves or anyone else: it is, then, the Voice of the Higher Self.

When we realize that we can transcend all the rampant negative energies in and around us by using our own courage and fortitude to do so, we can see our plan of action: We know what to do; we possess courage. When we do what needs to be done, we possess fortitude: we do it. We know that we can listen to that Voice within and are then able to carry through with its positive, beneficial advice.

- - - - -

Failure to pay close attention
to your soul's voice
calling loudly
will bring about
unnecessary pain,
deepening a void
that is supposed to be filling,
not left to chance,
but left for Destiny.

Last summer, they'd gone West on their vacation to meet with friends, cut loose, have some fun. Though it was an annual event, it was only the second time for her. But the first year had been a lot of fun, and she enjoyed the camaraderie of good friends, breathtaking scenery, and the all the happy times and unforgettable memories.

Along the way, they visited a few Native American sites, and it was then when she'd first noticed his fascination with rose quartz. She'd thought it odd for a guy who considered pink to be such a sissy color was now eagerly scrambling to buy it. He had bought quantities of stones in different sizes and shapes. He'd even purchased a long, beautiful rose quartz necklace for her after they'd reached their destination. And several months after they had returned home, he bought two huge rocks from the local pet store. They're supposed to go into an aquarium, he told her, but the price was so cheap! It was an ongoing love affair with the quartz.

It was also that summer when she had first noticed a drastic change in his behavior. Normally relaxed and easygoing, he sometimes became spiteful and irritable immediately before, and during the trip. During one part of the long drive, they were riding in two separate vehicles: she was with friends, while he drove theirs. He had taken some terrible chances when driving along the narrow mountain roads, recklessly passing the slower-moving trucks and trailers, barely missing the vehicles that sud-denly appeared in the oncoming lanes on the winding curves. She didn't say anything, however, because she somehow thought he knew what he was doing, despite his erratic actions. He'd always been a safe driver, so she figured he was in a hurry to get there.

And she thought everything would be all right when, later that day, he sat on the floor at the end of the bed in their motel, lamenting, what is happening to me?!

Your spirit has gone wild in these mountains, was her response. He'd been born and raised north of these mountains; she figured that he missed the area, but was unwilling to admit it to her. I don't belong here anymore, he'd told her, or something to that effect. I go where the jobs take us. . .

And he was all right for a couple of days, but after that, his strange behavior continued intermittently for the remainder of the vacation. Sometimes she had a hard time interpreting his odd, vague statements. He belittled her in front of their friends, or answered her in a snide tone, as though she should know better than to ask such "stupid" questions. But if his friends noticed any of this, they said nothing.

And then there were the times when he'd be fine.

- - -

Not quite knowing what to make of all this, she didn't. Period. It's just my imagination, she thought, believing that everything would return to normal once the vacation was over.

In the meantime, they rarely socialized with the others during the day. Instead, he preferred to drive alone with her through the mountains, stopping periodically to view the scenery, collect rocks, buy rose quartz, or simply cruise non-stop for hours. At night, she went to their room exhausted, confused by what she thought she had seen, frustrated in his change toward her and grateful for the refuge and solitude the four walls had offered. He would stay out late with their friends, into the early (and sometimes later) hours of the morning, and she'd get up and take long walks alone in the nearby woods or briefly visit with the others who were leaving to tour the area.

After they returned home, she decided not to go with him to the mountains again next year.

- - - - -

A Meditation:
Listening for the One Voice within

Here is a meditation and visualization exercise to enable us to listen for the one Voice of clarity inside ourselves:

As with all the exercises presented here, we begin by breathing deeply, inhaling the positive energies around us, and exhaling the negative from within. With each breath we take, we stop, think, and focus on our goal: finding the Voice within.

As we breathe methodically, not only do we balance, focus and center ourselves, but we also clear any stresses and problems resulting from the day's activities.

Once we have cleared ourselves, we can be rest assured that our first thought will be from Spirit; the second is usually us doubting ourself. After those two thoughts, any other thoughts, depending upon their quality and intent, are ours for fuller contemplation.

- - - - -

There are times that, despite our greatest and best intentions, our wants and desires tend to cloud us over, limiting our clear vision and inhibiting our hearing abilities. When this happens, we must wait for the fog to lift.

Here is a visualization to bring into meditation to help dissipate the fog:

It is summertime, and the weather was hot and humid;
however, it has just rained, and it is now cool.
The coolness of this summer rain has left the air fresh and clear.

Bring to your mind's eye a smooth, clear lake.
The waters are blue and calm, peaceful, and glassy.
As the sky becomes clearer, air begins to warm again, forming mists
which rise from the water's surface,
turning into white, steamy clouds.
These misty clouds hover, dancing over the lake.
As the mists rise, so rise the oppressive wants that have clouded us
over...

- - - - -

Complacency is dangerous

Just as may other things, complacency can be either beneficial or detrimental, depending upon how we perceive it and how we use it.

Complacency, when defined as satisfaction or an ease of mind, is not dangerous if we see this as being satisfied with the things about ourselves that we cannot change, manifested in one's physical appearance (good examples might be that we perceive ourselves to be too tall or too short, or the fact that we might need to wear corrective lenses for optimum vision), or one's mental abilities (such as when we are required to take a math class for school, but math is a struggle for us).

If we spend our time seeking to change the things about ourselves that cannot be changed, not only will we waste a lot of energy on the impossible, but we will only become miserable in the process as well. Instead, we can simply be satisfied in knowing who we are and knowing the nature of our limitations; thus we are able to gain self-acceptance. We simply learn to work with them and get on with our lives.

Complacency is dangerous, however, if we have been using it to shield ourselves from the situations or conditions in our lives we have either consciously, or subconsciously chosen to avoid or ignore altogether. When defined in terms of (ego) self-gratification and self-satisfaction, complacency then becomes self-serving, for it requires us to focus on the world through the eyes of our own wants and needs, distorting our awareness so that we will see only what we want to see, rather than when we objectively view the world and its inhabitants as they truly exist.

If or when this does happen to us, we might say that complacency, as viewed in this context, refers to the illusions we have built around ourselves, in which reality has no basis. If this type of complacency is our "reality," then we are lacking the awareness essential for our own spiritual survival.

This complacency is the type wherein we tell ourselves that we are satisfied with what we have accomplished in our lives, or that we are happy right where we are; perhaps we are telling ourselves that we are doing the best we can and utilizing our full abilities when in fact, deep down inside, either consciously or subconsciously, we know that we are not any of these things, that we are not doing these things, and we might be doing better but are holding ourselves back in some manner. In reality, we are limiting ourselves in some way and are either unable or unwilling to do something about it.

Through our own illusions, then, we have created a world in our minds that is meant to serve us and give us what we think we need, yet somehow that world can never provide for us, according to our expectations. Not only will it never give us enough, but it will not give us the something which we truly need, and that something is our own inner peace.

We can deceive ourselves for only so long, however. The soul knows its purpose, and that purpose is stored in our subconscious mind...

- - - - -

From the Subconscious into the Conscious Mind: from Misty Grey Shadows Into the White Light - Awareness is Now.

There comes a point in our lives when the illusions of our complacency are shattered in some manner. As we already know, timing is everything, and when the illusions are shattered, it is meant that we see the reality for what it is. Regardless of how we may have tried to avoid it, the Universe is now showing us what we need to see.

- - - - -

Staying right where we are

When things in our lives need changing, it is possible that we might remain complacent nevertheless, without awareness, without ever awakening, and without ever knowing that things might need to be changed for our betterment. We might always be content and self-satisfied, and in deluding ourselves with our own self-created illusions, we might miss knowing the true nature of our destiny.

But this occurrence is highly unlikely, for the soul always realizes its destiny, even if we do not consciously recognize it, or refuse to acknowledge it. Regardless of what our conscious might recognize or block, our subconscious always knows the soul's purpose, for the knowledge of the soul is embodied in the subconscious mind. An awakening of this type seems to move in the natural order of things, orchestrated by both timing and destiny. We can be assured, then, that when we become aware of our soul's destiny, we were meant to know at that time.

- - - - -

*Why did you buy all the rose quartz? she asked one sunny day.
It was the winter following the trip out West. The pink in the quartz reminded her of the way the sunlight had glistened on the snow outside. One huge rock sat in her study by the quartz necklace, and another rock was by the television in their bedroom. The little stones were in some invisible place elsewhere in the house.
Because rose quartz is known for its healing properties,
he had replied.
It heals wounds of the heart, she added.*

- - - - -

Free Will and Choice:
We want what the Universe wants

If we have come to a point where the circumstances in our lives as they exist now no longer seem to be working for us anymore, but we are unwilling to shatter our complacency because it seems to be an overwhelming task, then we need to remember two things: Not only is there peace when we get past the pain, but there is self-empowerment when we shatter our illusions as well.

We will know that when the down side hits us the next time, not only will we choose the path most beneficial for our self-esteem, good health and well-being, but we will also have the reason to pursue the best path for ourselves. From within comes a peace of mind that cannot be supplied by any external force or person around us.

Finally, when we have demonstrated our own sense of self-empowerment and self-esteem (we would only want the best for ourselves as we would for others), the Universe knows we are ready to meet our destiny, whatever that might be. And we just might be surprised to find that our destiny is the very same thing that made us feel happy and peaceful inside all along!

- - - - -

Exercises
To shatter the complacency
surrounding us. . .

. . .Self-Knowledge and Self-Awareness is Power.

- - - - -

Here is an exercise to help you to assess where you are right now, and where you would like to be in your spiritual development.

Before you commence this exercise, there are two things you need to do:

First, have some paper and a pen or pencil handy to jot down your impressions for the second part of this exercise;

then, begin by breathing deeply to cleanse any negative or judgmental energies that might have penetrated your conscious-ness during your waking hours. In doing so, you enable your first thought to be from Spirit.

As we remember, then, when we are open, free and clear of negativity, the first thought is always from Spirit, and the second is your self doubting your first thought. Focus on the positive as you inhale, and expel the negative as you exhale, clearing your mind, while relaxing your body.

Once you have done this, three things need to be considered:

1. First, list five (5) things that you would like to see changed as

your material reality, meaning your own belief system. As you contemplate your material reality, consider the following questions:

* What do you believe about yourself and the world around you?

* Do these things in which you base your beliefs cause you to feel happy or sad?

* How did you come to these beliefs?

* Are these beliefs beneficial to both yourself and others, as well as the world around you?

* Why do you believe these things?

Be honest with your answers. Remember, this exercise is for your own personal assessment, for not only will they help you with this portion of the exercise, but with the two following as well. You do not have to justify your answers to any other person, but only to the Higher Self within.

2. After you have thoroughly contemplated the questions and your answers above, list five (5) things that you would affirm, that you can have, but not through manipulative (ego-based) effort. This means that we would only want something that will be for our own betterment or for the benefit of others, without hurting anyone else in the process, including ourselves. In other words, these are things that would occur in the Divine order. Examples might be a lifestyle or change/modification of a habit or behavioral pattern; perhaps it might be eliminating judgmental or self-defeating thinking; or a spiritual goal, such as a greater tolerance of others, or a greater self-love. Begin with such phrases as I believe that, or I will do my best to, or something else about which you feel strongly.

3. Finally, list five (5) things that you have already manipulated

with the ego self, that you are now willing to release. As you might expect, such a willingness implies commitment, so be certain that you are serious about following through with these things.

Once you have a good idea of what you believe, what you want and what you are willing to release, you have started to create a road map to your own specific needs and requirements. Even though each of us is from one Soul, one Light, we are all as different as the falling snowflakes in wintertime. Each of us has a unique and special contribution to give to the world and to ourselves, regardless of how great or small it might seem to ourselves and to others. It is up to us to know what that contribution is, however. This is the first step in our process toward self-awareness.

- - - - -

PART II

WIND:
TRANSITIONS

We have been programmed
to desensitize Ourselves

Standing at the kitchen door early Saturday night, she heard a loud thump, followed by a crash and then a shatter. She knew that some cherished piece of glass was now only a half-forgotten memory.

Oh, man, he said turning slowly around, and she looked around him and saw that the hall cabinet where they'd kept her shotglass collection was hanging by a single nail. The shotglasses were now scattered on the kitchen floor. Whatever had broken had shattered into a thousand glistening pieces.

Are you okay? She asked.

Yeah, he responded, and then lapsed into silence.

She grabbed a broom and instructed him to get the vacuum.

Should I say something about the amount he's had to drink? she wondered. Silently, she began sweeping, not knowing what else to do. They'd discussed his drinking before, and if he saw that he'd had too much, he didn't say anything about it now. But she felt that the situation spoke for itself.

He had returned with the vacuum and was doing his best to stay out of her way. Interestingly, only one shotglass broke, but it was the one he'd brought her from Denver, from his recent business trip to the home office. He'd always expressed his dissatisfaction about both his job and the fact that one day they might have to move to Denver, a place for whatever reason, he had never wanted to live.

Hey, only one shotglass broke, she said. It's the one from Denver. Continuing her avoidance of the subject, she asked, How much have you eaten today?

Oh, just snacks, he replied.

Maybe you need to eat something, she said, resisting her screaming impulse to just say it: Maybe you shouldn't be drinking so much!

Instead, they began to discuss the significance of the broken Denver shotglass, and what perhaps it might mean. And all the while, she was ignoring his comments on how cute she was and how lucky he was to have her and all the while, she wanted to scream and say Damnit! Look at what you're doing to yourself.

But how would he respond?

She assumed that he'd respond as he always did, You're right. I drink too much, and let it go at that. And then he'd say,

But I love you. You give my life meaning. I couldn't do this without you.

She couldn't stand to hear it. Perhaps it was the guilt. Perhaps it's something I'm not ready to face. The sudden thought surprised her.

He was supposed to go on another fishing trip with a friend, so he left after telling how much he loved her and how lucky he was to have her in his life.

- - -

The next morning, she awoke slowly, delighted to be alone in bed with nothing but her books around her. She took her time with her morning routine, relishing the silence and tranquil energies around the place. But last night weighed heavily upon her mind, and she didn't know what to think, what to do about it. Putting the issue on the back burner, she went down to the basement to do laundry.

She was closing the basement door from the den to the bar when she heard a clank, then a tink. Wondering, what now? she quickly spotted the beer can that seemed to have jumped from atop the old-fashioned wall phone and had landed squarely in the wastebasket below it.

What does that tell me?! she thought quickly.

Time to say something to him. Time to admit to herself that she hadn't said anything before because she was hiding from both herself and from him: She used his drinking for the camouflage to hide from her own self and her self-destructive habits.

She would have to let go of her fears, step out there in faith and just do it. Say something for the both of them, but with dignity and respect.   To remain silent would resolve nothing. Do it for us both.

- - -

It was not until Monday morning, just before she left for work that he mentioned the incident Saturday night and the broken shotglass. Sheepishly he said, I'm really tired this morning! Guess I'm paying for having too much fun.

But there was no time to talk right then. He was heading out of town that morning; his bags were open and waiting to be packed. There was only enough time for her to say goodbye and hurry out the door.

Sitting in the quiet of her office, she remembered his words and thought she'd catch him before he left town. She was alone here and could think without any distractions or interruptions. If she could call and talk to him, perhaps they could discuss it and clear the air.

Dialing his number, she was amazed to hear his voice at the other end. Usually, he was away from his office, checking his mail, catching up on the others' weekend activities, handling last-minute details.

Just wanted to say goodbye, and have a safe trip, she began.

Good to hear your voice! he said softly, as though he missed her. Or perhaps he didn't want anyone else to hear their conversation. Or maybe because he'd wanted to say something else to her before she'd hurried out the door?

I'm glad you said something about this weekend and "having too much fun." That incident with the cabinet and shotglass really worried me. . ."

She was feeling stronger already, and paused.

Oh, that part didn't bother me, he said nonchalantly, and in a louder tone, obviously picking up on her nuance. Could have lost my balance drunk or sober, and I was in a hurry.

Good point. She herself was naturally clumsy: her lack of coordination had been a running joke over the years.

Feeling that the subject was now closed, her mind immediately switched gears, and they began discussing other things, the incident temporarily forgotten.

- - -

Later, she contemplated his response. It wasn't as though he was unaware of his drinking; he himself had mentioned it before, and a few times, they'd even discussed it. There were two conversations she specifically remembered. The first one, when she'd asked him, Why do you drink so much? he replied, It's easy to get carried away. . .

To her, that was an honest, rational response. It is easy to get carried away. It would be possible to change the action, but only if he wanted to change it.

But another time, many years ago, she'd asked that same question. It was late at night, and they were sitting at opposite ends of the dining room table. He answered slowly, sadly,

21

Because the world is such an ugly place when I'm sober. . .

That was an answer for which she had no argument. How could she change his perception of the world that he saw?

But since neither situation would be addressed, she let the issue drop altogether. She figured that if she said nothing, it wasn't as though she were holding something back that he hadn't already heard or didn't already know. Apparently, his drinking was a problem, but only to her.

It is I who must change. If I pressed the issue, he might fix the symptoms, but the problem would still be there: he'd be sober, but still in a place that he perceives as miserable. What good would that do for either of them?

She suddenly realized that if she thought something needed to be fixed, she'd better take a good look at herself. Why should she try to change him if he didn't want to change himself? What was he holding on to?

To what was she clinging?

She thought she had been happy, and loving him had made her happy. She wanted him to be happy and love her, too. But love and happiness were two different issues: though he had loved her, he wasn't happy now, nor was he, even when they first met.

How clouded were their minds when, many years ago, they'd first proclaimed their love for each other?

Regardless, it was now beyond her control.

Finally, she realized that nobody can make anybody else happy. He would have to be happy first, just as she should have been, for it is through the self, from the Self, that all love flows. Then, whatever love they had felt for each other would only have enhanced the happiness they already had within themselves.

Suddenly she realized that when they first met, she lacked in self-esteem. He was her proof to the world that somebody loved her. She had finally proven herself acceptable when she had long believed that she was unlovable and unacceptable.

She wondered whether he believed that she was the reason for his happiness; in his own misery, did he need validation for his existence in a world in which he didn't want to live?

Regardless of his issues, however, she only needed to resolve hers. She needed find her own way; she must no longer depend upon him for that kind of validation. Despite his own problems, he was a good person, and he didn't deserve any more baggage than he was already carrying.

How could she have seen all that without the help of her wise friend?

- - -

I can see perfectly well.
Which way am I headed?!

From early on, we were taught to throw up smokescreens. But if each of us is still doing this, who is shining the Light ahead?

We're missing a piece of our destiny.

- - - - -

Despite the changes going on her life, reminiscing about her first trip out West felt good to her. But things do have their shadow side, she thought, and she was surprised at how easily she recognized them when she was paying attention to them. Before, she had remembered it as only a happy event, but now, she closed her eyes and began to breathe deeply, this time carefully viewing every detail about it.

And when she was done, she was amazed how much she'd actually recognized even back then, but had refused to acknowledge it. . .

- - -

Because this was the first long vacation she'd had in years, it would automatically make it one of the greatest! She was going to do things she didn't normally do, most important of which was leaving all her responsibilities behind for awhile. It meant putting that flavored creamer in her coffee they'd get in the convenience shops, rather than watching her fat and caloric intake as she normally did at home. It was the Great Adventure where every one of their friends felt a special bond with each other, long after the last ones had finally returned to the city. It was driving sometimes through treacherous, unpredictable rains and heavy thunderstorms.

She could feel the danger even back then.

∧ ∧ ∧

Arriving in these mountains had a special feeling all its own. It greeted, and surrounded her as they began to ascend the first narrow pass, which was marked by the young scrubs of the many pine trees clinging off the sides of the warm brown hills. The very air seemed to be beckoning her, saying to her, You have finally arrived.

She felt her spirit beginning to transform. She believed that it would learn to fly here, at first dipping close to the mountains, touching the trees and rocks, and then begin to head skyward to dance and dip closer to Mother Earth.

Dance and dip and fly. . .

And then, after the dance would finally end, her spirit would find its power and soar skyward on its own path toward the Sun.

- - -

But even then, she sensed the shadows surrounding those mountains. There was a heaviness in her chest, as if she were she were trying inhale deeply, yet could not. She also felt a strange sense of tears, though she hadn't actually cried any. This feeling was also accompanied by a desperation that she figured must have been perpetuated by the many Native American spirits still wandering aimlessly through and around these mountains. It was the type of feeling that left the pit of her stomach heavy with sorrow, and the unshed tears were somehow choking her. She would experience the same feeling a couple of months later, when she would attend her first pauwau in a nearby community close to their home.

Although she realized that she by nature was quite emotional anyway (he'd always thought she was overemotional), she was in fact part Native American by blood on her mother's side. But she also felt that this was more than just an emotional overreaction to the energies that lingered about these mountains; there was something else about this place that she simply couldn't explain.

Yet she believed that her feelings far transcended that empathic bond of ancestry, for despite her lineage, she knew very little about Native history. He, on the other hand, was the expert in Native history and ways. Not only had he been here several times before (enough to consider his visits a "tradition" within their own circle of friends), but he'd learned much on his own over the years, long before he'd ever met her. He was, in fact, more Native than she would, or ever could be.

But this was a mystical place, she felt, and it kept 'em coming in droves, returning year after year to experience the mysterious energies that held a different significance to each who took the annual pilgrimage here. There was no other place in the country, the world, that was quite like this, and each "pilgrim" knew it. People were born here, people would always vacation here.

And there would always be some would actually die here.

Some would get crazy; it happened every year. Others might lose control, possibly while traveling along the treacherous winding roads higher up on the passes.

And even then, she felt that some would ultimately be reborn.

- - -

Broadening your perception and listening to your intuition sets you on the Path.

Having recognized the nature of our material reality, what we might desire to change, and what we are willing to release, we have begun to penetrate our complacency and have taken a step toward a greater self-awareness. With this information, we are now ready to embark upon a journey to eliminate our complacency and replace it with this new awareness.

If we had any difficulty at all with the previous exercise, it could be that we have been hiding in the shadows for too long, sequestered from reality and any semblance of awareness. If this were so, it would not be surprising, for the process of daily life and its activities can in itself be overwhelming sometimes. We may have been so caught up in the process of doing that sometimes we forget the purpose behind what we do. And sometimes, we are so busy doing, that we may not even be paying attention to what it is we are doing!

In the midst of all the noise of our daily activities, we may forget that they are somehow related to the lessons we need to learn, as we progress along our path. Although we may have paused to catch a faint impression that there's something more to what we are doing, and had started to question it, another feeling right behind the first one may have told us to get back to the task at hand, urging us along, especially if that first thought was interfering with what we were doing.

Any faint stirring, restless feelings or impressions that we are unable to specifically define, originate in the subconscious mind, the seat of our intuition (the sixth sense). As we may remember, the subconscious portion of our mind is more susceptible to both the internal and external stimuli around us, which is why we need to keep this part of the mind active and alert. However, since we are more aware of the thoughts generated from the conscious, or everyday reasoning mind, we tend to base our observations on those impressions, rather than those obtained from the subconscious mind.

If our intuition, or subconscious mind seems to be telling us something, then, we need to pay better attention to its impressions. Our much-needed awareness awaits us there.

- - - - -

. . .I don't have a choice. I have to work. We need money to survive.

It was the same old argument, with the same old lines, same old issues. Why she managed to trigger this fight—she felt she'd had a substantial part in this one—she had no idea. But it had started nevertheless, and she was going to add her two cents' worth before it was finished.

No. We don't need money to survive. You have choices, and you made them. You have chosen to need money, and you've chosen to work in order to get that money. Work is an option. You could rob banks or seek financial assistance, or you could even win the lottery, fat chance! And if you don't feel money is necessary, then you could move away from the city and all its responsibilities, barter or live off the land, or both.

And they began to debate all the other issues.

It seemed that each time they began the same old argument,

something different emerged. Yet she always interjected that happiness issue, for to her, it was important. For him, work was not an option, it was a requirement, and happiness was unrelated. But for this go-round, it wasn't whether or not the job itself was what he enjoyed, but what he felt he was wasting when he was working at it. Work is a waste of my time, he stated flatly.

Then what would you do with all that spare time? she asked. This was new issue to her and she was confused. Her confusion made her uncomfortable. Did he mention this before, and she missed it because she hadn't been paying attention?

I'm sorry, she said. I thought weren't happy because of your job. Do you care about being happy? she asked, wondering if that was now an issue.

Of course! he replied, as if it were already understood.

Aha! When did this happen? But she was not about to get sidetracked. What makes you happy?

You make me happy, he said.

Still determined not to get off the subject, she left that alone for the moment, too. What would you do if you didn't have to work all day?

Whatever I wanted to do, he quipped.

And what would that be?

Whatever I felt like at the time.   We could just jump on an airplane, and -

Wait a minute! What is this we stuff?! she interjected.

I want us to do things together! Don't you want to do these things with me?!

No! I like working. It gives me a routine, and I feel that I'm doing something constructive. While my job isn't what I want to do the rest of my life, there's a purpose to it. I just haven't figured it out, but that's okay; I will eventually. She chuckled at her own confusion, and then continued.

Besides, you don't need me to make you happy. Remember last October when we were waiting in line for the movies with friends and you mentioned our trip out West last summer? You said, I went out West, but I had to come back early, because I got sick. I was there, too, you know! So where does this we stuff come from now?

You mean you actually remember all this from last October?!

I'll probably have to hear this for several hundred more times! He looked hurt, apparently sidestepping the issue about the I (singular), versus the we (collective).

Seeing his hurt look, she softened a bit.

That's not the point I'm trying to make, she said gently. All I'm saying is that you're telling me how you want us to be together, do things together, when in fact you're doing this stuff by yourself, whether I'm there or not!

She paused for a moment, thinking about how he would take off for the slopes without her tomorrow, thrilled at the prospect of an afternoon outing with his friends.

He was silent then. Finally, he spoke.

I don't like it when we fight like this, he said.

If there's something wrong, we need to talk about it, she responded.

Now it was her turn to be silent. There was nothing more to say for now.

She was now late for work. She hurried to the kitchen, grabbed her lunch, stuffed it into her bag and put her coffee mug next to the sink. Silently he followed her to the kitchen, and then out the door to watch her climb into her car and drive away.

- - -

Hours later, in the safe haven and quiet of her own office, she thought about their argument. She was amazed that she no longer felt bad it its aftermath, as she would have before. Perhaps it was because the arguments were becoming more frequent; perhaps it was because there was really nothing to feel bad about, and because she was now beginning to realize it. They were two totally different people, and it seemed that he was beginning to recognize it, too. It was a painful experience for him, just as it had been for her.

She realized that his conscious words belied what was going on in his subconscious mind. Yet his actions clearly demonstrated his true heart. She could now see that they did not match at all. These were the words that would not come.

When you no longer need each other, you can let each other go.

Her friend's words indicated that this would not be an overnight process.

How different they were when they first met! But back then, it didn't matter; love was the only thing that mattered at that time. If they had love, everything else would fall into place. What else was there besides love?

How they had changed over the years! Did they even know each other anymore? She searched for the words that would express her feelings. Finally, they came:

I was I; he was he.
I became him; he became me.
But are we happy?
And who are We?

She had no answer.

- - - - -

Tuning into the Higher Self

Our greatest task at this time is to attain clarity. Knowing this, we realize that we must learn to pay better attention to the impressions originating from our subconscious mind. We can attain this by tuning into the Higher Self.

In order to contact the Higher Self, we begin with prayer and meditation.

- - - - -

Prayer is asking. . .

When we pray, we seek to communicate to a Higher Source.

Whether we seek guidance for a challenge or situation we face, protection or forgiveness, or whether we might simply be asking our Higher Source to accept our gratitude or thanks, we are in some way invoking or asking for the attention of the Higher Source within us.

The most important aspect to remember about prayer, then, is that we need to ask the right questions, so that we will obtain the answers we truly seek.

...Meditation is listening

Unlike prayer, the purpose of meditation is contemplation: we have determined the issues or aspects of a situation for which we seek assistance, and we now listen for an answer. And when we listen for the answer, we employ the total harmony of the mind-body-spirit connection, and align ourselves with our Higher Source.

With either prayer or meditation, we must remember that we seek results only in the Divine Order of things, and we always begin our questions with this phrase, while in prayer or meditation. It is also most important to thank our Higher Source for the wisdom imparted to us.

It is also important that we do not seek anything for anyone other than ourselves, as much as we might like to help them, although we are allowed to ask for protection from the Divine on their behalf. This is so because it is not meant that we deprive anyone else of the lessons that they need to learn, and the responsibilities they must assume, just as it is not for them to assume ours.

As we seek to gain control of our own lives, then, we must step back and allow others to do the same.

- - - - -

Awareness in the present:
in and around Us

When we determined the thoughts which motivate us while working with the meditation in the previous section, we became aware of what was going on inside both our conscious and subconscious mind: we sought answers to our questions, quietly contemplating and pondering our possible answers. We waited and listened to the responses from our Higher Source.

A second type of awareness is attained by observing our immediate physical surroundings. The following exercise will help you attain this awareness. Many times, we think we are paying full attention to everything around us, but are later surprised to find that we somehow missed an important detail that was out in plain sight.

- - - - -

For the next thirty minutes, practice being fully aware of your surroundings and the objects in it:

Look around you, first scanning the area to determine what you can see. Then, look closer, carefully observing everything: describe each object in your view. Note the colors of each object, their textures, shapes and sizes. What relationship, if any, do they have to the objects immediately surrounding them? Take another look, and then close your eyes. Can you recall what you have just seen? In your mind's eye, do you see the details as when your eyes were open?

Next, listen closely to each of the sounds that immediately jump out at you. (You might find that this is easier to do when your eyes are closed, to eliminate any visual distractions.) What types of noises do you hear? Are they humming sounds? Staccato? Strident? Soft? How many are there? Does one cause the other? Are they occurring simultaneously, or intermittently?

Think of a sentence, and then say it aloud.

Listen to the tone of your voice, the words you say, and consider the intent behind them. When you do this, you become aware not only of the physical sound of your voice, but also the tone and intent as reflected from within you.

Now, pay attention to your physical position.

Are you sitting? Standing? Lying down?

When you are completely still, can you feel your heart beating? Can you feel your breath each time you inhale and exhale? And as you breathe, do you become aware of any odors, such as the newly-mown grass if someone is mowing the lawn outside, or the smells of food if a meal is being prepared inside? Are you wearing cologne or perfume?

Breathe deeper. Do you taste anything in your mouth?

- - - - -

When you have completed this exercise, gently bring your mind back to the immediate reality. You will be amazed at how much is going on that sometimes isn't noticed!

Try to remember as many details as you can, and then write

them down. Record this information with the date and time. If you do this exercise for about a week, you may determine the part of the day your when senses might be sharper.

Not only will this exercise sharpen your awareness, but it will help you with your memory as well.

And if you found that you had any difficulty concentrating, don't despair. Just do the best you can, and then try again later. When you continue, you will improve over time.

- - - - -

Human emotions and Soul emotions

There are two types of emotions we are capable of feeling: those originating from the aspect of human nature, and those coming from the soul. As we might anticipate, the emotions experienced by our human nature are bound in certain responsibilities and conditions, whereas those from the soul have no boundaries.

The human emotions are a blend between the human mind and the heart, and for this reason, they tend to be limiting: influenced by the conscious mind, the human heart has its frailties, and places certain expectations and requirements which are imposed by the particular mindset of that individual. Human emotions, then, are governed by certain boundaries, structures and conditions. A good example of these traits is the phrase, "I will love you, but only if you love me back." (In other words, I want my love to be justifiable in my own eyes and validated by others who see my love for you.)

As humans, we seek recognition from both our selves and from others for what we perceive to be our right actions; the external sources upon we have imposed our limits must provide it for us, so that we may feel rightly feel justified in our feelings and perspectives. And because our perspectives are based upon the circumstances and outcomes surrounding the situations and events of past-present-future, the human heart also has a physical memory.

Soul emotions, on the other hand, are limitless, having essentially no boundaries or expectations placed upon them. The love for others that we humans feel from the soul flows through us from the Source, or our Higher Self. We are capable of feeling this Love for the sake of Love itself: this Love loves us for the essence of who we are, as souls from the same Source, and not for what we do, as manifested in our actions.

This Love is also one that requires the listening attitude. To attain this, we remember that sometimes we must distance ourselves from our own human, and sometimes selfish (ego-based) desires. Hence, the memories possessed by the soul are not those of convenience; rather, they are those based upon Truth as seen through the eyes of the Universe.

If any boundaries, however, seemed to be imposed by this Love, they are actually not, for these "boundaries" are in reality defined by courtesy, as we wish only the best for someone else.

Such emotions might indicate that we become pacifists, yet such is not the case: we are allowed to be assertive, but not aggressive, for we seek to protect and defend ourselves in the event that someone is trying to harm us, just as we would seek to protect our children or other loved ones from harm.

It must be clarified that defending or protecting another from unwarranted aggression is not assuming another's responsibility, especially if it is requested. There is a distinction between aggression in that aggression, as a forced circumstance, is imposed upon another, often against the free will and choice of that individual. Responsibilities, however, are either assigned or willingly undertaken by another; Hence, the victim may be unable or incapable of helping himself or herself.

We are allowed, then, to protect ourselves, and others, if required, from the malice and intent of others' lower ego-based emotions, at the time we need to do so.

The soul, as manifested within our physical and mental bodies, then, is expressed by the qualities we know as the human attributes, which includes a recollection of right action. The soul does indeed have a memory, but what little memory the soul does possess is not one of convenience, however, for if we feel we have wronged someone, the soul emotions would require that we face it and seek forgiveness as required. Such are the qualities of Unconditional Love, and when we seek this Love to manifest itself, we are striving to attain all the Universe has to offer, in the Divine Order of things, or for the Higher Purpose.

- - - - -

Since he hadn't called to let her know, she knew that he would be coming home late from work. He had only recently been calling to let her know when he was going to be late, so if he called now, she considered it unusual anyway. Over the years, she'd asked him repeatedly to call as a matter of courtesy, but he'd rarely complied; apparently he hadn't shared that opinion. Now, it didn't matter anymore to her whether he called or not. It was just the way things were.

Predictably, he was angry and upset when he finally arrived. But lately, the anger was more intense and seemed to be mingled with a sense of urgency and frustration. Losing himself in the process of his job, of acting, thinking, doing, and commiserating with his friends and coworkers was no longer sufficient to quell his restlessness. His grievances were so typical of the many others suffering from the same frustrations: too many added responsibilities, increased production quotas factored into his job description, layoffs despite exemplary job performance. All that seemed to matter anymore was the bottom line. But where does all the money go after so many workers are laid off?

And she responded with her stock answer: Nothing is going to change, and you know that. Perhaps you might consider a different career altogether. What would you do, if you could do anything you wanted for a living, and enjoy doing it?

Which initiated the same discussion as of late. It began with I don't know, and continued with her rejoinder of What would make you happy? to which he would respond with Winning a million dollars in the lottery, and then she'd say That's not realistic, and from there it would go downhill: he, venting about the job he was frightened of losing, but didn't want to keep anyway, yet didn't know what he really wanted to do in life, and apparently not willing to consider the possibilities. Predictably, it always went nowhere. And in her opinion, he seemed unwilling to consider what actually would make him happy.

But this time, the argument took a sharp turn when he asked

her: Are you happy with your job?

Yes, she immediately responded. I'm happy with it. The people are nice to me, I have a beautiful office, and I have my own private phone line.

Although I could be making a lot more money elsewhere doing the same thing, I have great benefits. My hours are stable, and right now, I can develop my own personal interests. It's not about money anymore, it's about doing the things I want to do. Yes, I'm happy, she repeated, and then froze. In her ears, she was beginning to sound like a whiny little kid.

Grow up. Get a grip. If you don't know how to worry, you aren't an adult! screamed some disembodied voice inside her head.

But worse yet, she actually felt like a little kid, smiling into the bleak world of Reality, looking up at the stars while sinking inch by inch in the quagmire of her dead-end job, where she'd chosen to stay until her health became better. She was embarrassed because it was only the little things that were right about that job. In her ears, it sounded as though she had refused to acknowledge the real problem by taking comfort in the pretty things around her.

Suddenly, she remembered the childhood she'd chosen to forget, when her caregivers told her not to act happy. How could you be happy when life was so difficult? they told her. To be an adult, you must learn to worry. You can be happy only when you have nothing to worry about.

While her child's heart realized that they were teaching her to be a responsible, productive member of society, her child's mind believed that misery was the badge of adulthood and that her happiness must dance to the music of her circumstances.

But as an adult, her life had never free of its difficult situations, though she had her share of good times. When could she ever be truly happy?

Suddenly, it dawned on her that she wasn't that little kid anymore. She was grown now, and as an adult, she now recognized her capacity to choose: she could make the changes happen if she wanted. But she would have to live with them, and her choices would be beneficial to all involved. . .

Her thoughts were interrupted by his next question: Why do

you care whether I am happy?

She lost sight of her own perspectives as she proceeded to answer his question.

- - -

It was not until much later that she contemplated the very nature of the question itself, for her first thought was that it was asked out of sincerity. He truly did not understand why his happiness would matter to anyone, let alone her.

The one Obvious Answer for two married people who were loved each other was Because I love you and I care about you. But because she wasn't thinking on that level, the Obvious Answer hadn't occurred to her.

So her first words were: because I'm from California, and it takes five of us to change a light bulb so we can all share the experience!

He smiled at her feeble attempts to joke as she continued, Because all human beings are entitled to be happy, and you're a member of the human race, regardless of your dissatisfaction you might have with them right now.

After he'd considered her answer, he turned away, silenced.

- - -

But it was only after she finished that she began to wonder about the Obvious answer: What about the love they had shared for each other?

But the love she did have for him was beginning to wear a little thin with all this constant bickering and his constant dissatisfaction combined with their collective frustrations, and it seemed that the Obvious Answer no longer applied to them. And if this love was so Obvious, why did he have to ask in the first place?

At that very moment she realized that she had nothing to do with his happiness. She never had, and she never would be able to make him happy. From the very beginning, his dream was to move away from civilization, just live in a little cabin in the woods, self-sufficient and sequestered. She could picture him there, too, with a long, full beard, even though his hair had been short at that time, and he was clean-shaven. And for awhile, he had gone away, close to his childhood home, close to the wilderness in which he'd grown up. But he had given up that life and had returned to the city to marry her after only four months back home.

For years after that, his joke to new people he'd meet was that she'd "blindsighted him," and he came back to her. And every so often, he'd repeat the dream, then quickly add that he was happy, that with her was where he'd wanted to be.

But she never looked in his eyes to see if it was the truth, his truth.

Now she knew.

It was then she'd learned that love simply was not enough: she was not, nor would she alone ever make him happy.

- - -

Perhaps he was surprised that anyone else could care about whether he was happy or not. Or, was he wondering why she hadn't said The Obvious?

But if it were so Obvious, why did he have to ask in the first place?

But whatever he might have been thinking, she hadn't lied.

And she realized that their love of the Obvious kind had long ago passed, and the only love that remained was that from the Universe.

- - - - -

Unconditional Acceptance

One of the most difficult issues we face is that we must accept the situations in which we find ourselves, as they presently stand, for in accepting them, we begin to release them, thereby allowing us to progress on our path. Acceptance of this type is known as an unconditional acceptance.

Acceptance does not mean that we should stop trying to amicably resolve any negative situations we might face, or that we should run from the difficult challenges in our lives, if they can be resolved without harm to others. Rather, in accepting the situation as it stands, we release ourselves from the self-imposed limitations of the ego-based emotional reactions that immobilize and disable us from right, beneficial and constructive action. We enhance our opportunities to obtain the best outcome possible for all involved.

Releasing ourselves from our emotional reactions not only frees us to take right action, but it also enables us to move beyond our

present circumstances. We find that when we begin to release them, all that we desire from the Divine will ultimately begin to fall into place. The Universe sees that we are ready, committed and have the fortitude to handle the responsibilities and greater challenges that accompany our advanced wisdom.

- - - - -

Rise above the anger...

Probably one of the most limiting emotions that inhibits our capacity for unconditional acceptance is that of anger, for not only is anger the cause of much externally destructive behavior upon others, but it is also the cause of much inner self-turmoil and destruction, for in many, it is the only emotion they might have knowingly experienced. While we cannot see the inner turmoil of the many who appear to be calm (even to themselves), their anger boils in what might be considered the "rage below the surface." It is possible, then, to be angry and not even recognize its symptoms.

Another reason that anger is such a destructive emotion is because, if we have been unaware of our feelings for a long time, we might find that the first emotion to surface is anger, for it is the only one that can be definitively expressed. Usually, anger of this type is an acknowledgment and awareness of lost time and faded illusions.

Not only does anger indicate a sense of justification in the eyes of the person feeling angry, regardless of how inappropriate or unjustified the anger might seem to others, but anger is also closely related to a variety of other emotions, such as depression or grief, because its roots are based in that same sense of justification.

To release any anger then, would be the first major step in eliminating more than one destructive emotion. This will be accomplished if we first realize that we are angry, if this is the case. Such an acknowledgment will enable us to begin moving past the pain that keeps us mired in the place where we presently find ourselves.

Once we realize that we are angry, we then need to realize that the reality in which we lived before we awakened to the Now, no longer exists, and is therefore no longer appropriate to who we are now. We know, too, that anger is a self-destructive force whose negative energies will only damage us in the long run if they are not released.

While there are many ways in which one might release anger, one of the first basic steps can be to recognize the fact that, regardless of anger's origin, or the masks that anger wears, we must place it in the Light and rise above it, for darkness cannot follow Light.

- - - - -

...below the anger lies grief.

Just as anger can be a destructive emotion marked by its intensity, grief on its own merits can be just as intense in its sorrow. When we remove the mask of anger or other emotions that might have been buried in our anger, we have effectively disabled it and rendered it powerless: we have exposed it to the Light. Anger then loses its power and its structure, and we are left with grief.

As an acknowledgment of loss, be it either a loss of time, a recognition of unfulfilled expectations, or a realization that we cannot change the outcome of results from an event that has already transpired, or might be currently happening in our lives, grief might be considered a finality because we have acknowledged a situation for what it is and are now responding to our awareness of the circumstances which have caused the anger: we are no longer hiding them in darkness.

As a finality, grief is a also termination of the illusions we might have held as a future reality: at this point, we are left with nothing more except emptiness and perhaps a heavy heart.

But with this emptiness and heartache comes a promise of healing and regeneration: what is empty will fill again, and what might have hit bottom will again rise to the top. We can take comfort in the fact that there is peace when we move beyond the pain, and Light when we step out of the darkness.

- - - - -

A meditation to release grief

The following meditation will enable us to relax, focus, and let go of the grief that keeps us bound to our present behaviors and mindset. This meditation is more effective if you sit, either in a chair, or on the floor, with your spine erect.

As you sit quietly, begin by breathing deeply. Throughout this exercise, remember that as you breathe, you are inhaling the positive energies and exhaling the negative influences that keep you imprisoned in this grief.

When you feel that you are completely calm, focused and centered, feel the White, healing Light above you, shining through the top of your head, through the center of your spine and down through your body and all around you, completely covering you in its warm, comforting Light. Gradually relax each part of your body as the Light moves along your spine.

As you continue breathing, feel your breath moving through your body. Feel the warmth flowing through and around you, and the visualize the grief that has kept you a prisoner from your true Self as a hard, dead shell. The warm Light is penetrating it, cracking the shell.

As the shell cracks, it begins to crumble away, falling into pieces around you. Finally, the pieces transform into a soft grey mist which begins to rise all around you, retreating beyond the Light, and slowly evaporating into the air.

The air around you is now brighter than before and pure with the healing White Light in and around you. Nothing else matters now; nothing more can harm you.

Continue to breathe deeply for a few more minutes, gently focusing on the White Light in and around you as you inhale and exhale.

When you are ready, gradually open your eyes, feeling refreshed and lighter.

As you continue your day, remember that the Light is always

around you. Periodically remind yourself that with each breath you take, you are inhaling the energies of that Healing White Light, and releasing the negative influences.

- - - - -

Lost effort, lost time?

As we continue upon our individual spiritual path, we find that much of the time, we perceive our situations, circumstances and other people from the Universal perspective: we see things from a sense of harmlessness for everyone. We then feel that we are progressing smoothly.

But we humans sometimes fall prey to the perceptions filtered through the lower, ego-based conscious mind; we might get sidetracked and march along the path with a skewed perspective of self-righteousness and self-justification. We might feel that ours is the only opinion that matters and that we have been unjustly wronged.

When this ego-based mind perception begins to creep in, disabling our sense of Universal justice, effectively derailing our good intentions and leaving us with a sense of frustration and hopelessness with our spiritual progress, we might feel that our earlier efforts were wasted and we wonder if we've made any progress at all.

While we have, of course, since we're further along the path than we were previously, we can better see this when we return to Square One and begin again by cleansing our spirit.

- - - - -

Sometimes, we need to step back and listen.

Despite the fact that we sometimes get lost along the way, the Universe is very compassionate nevertheless. To help us get back on track, we are offered a cleansing of the spirit, which can be as simple and effective as a Spring rain.

As entities with highly telepathic abilities, we humans not only become mired in our own lower mind-based consciousness at times, but we can also pick up the disparate energies floating around us as well. Cleansing, then, becomes a continual process: Just as frequently as rain falls in Springtime, we get that many chances to refresh and renew our spirit.

- - - - -

Trust your Instincts.

Our instincts originate in our subconscious mind. When we do pause, step back and listen, we open ourselves to these senses, allowing that spiritual cleansing process to heal us.

The process of listening is actually a simple one: to begin, all we need to do is clear our minds. But we do have free will and choice, and we can make this process as simple as that Spring rain, or we can make it as complicated and as analytical as a college calculus course for a junior high student.

The choice is ours.

- - - - -

It was now early Spring, and her emotional barometer seemed to rise and fall with the tides. She wasn't certain what she was seeing in their house any anymore, so she just drifted along, hoping that things would quickly change, angry when they did not, and finally accepting whatever occurred in the Now. Something was withholding any kind of change right now. Whatever it was, she would have to wait.

For the good of all. . .

- - - - -

The lesson is in the Now.

When we realize that we truly are where we need to be and that we need to learn the lessons presented before us, we begin to release the inhibiting mindset of the ego self. And in doing so, it all begins to fall into place.

And as we are already well aware, the key word to all of this, is embodied in the word, beginning. The inhibiting mindset has been impressed upon us ever since we were old enough to learn the socially correct way of doing things. Granted, many of these ways are based out of courtesy and consideration of others, and they are indeed beneficial. Other ways, however, are based in illusions, deception and a sense of separation from the spiritual aspect of ourselves, and these ways are the ones that can prove detrimental.

In releasing the negative aspects of our socialization which have desensitized and separated us from Spirit, we need to remember that this is an ongoing, or a continual process. When our lower nature begins to die, the new, better aspect of ourselves will not all come at once. And, depending upon our own individual lessons, we may not see any profound changes for awhile.

Regardless of the nature of the changes, or the expediency of its manifestation, however, it will take time.

- - - - -

The passage of each day finally brought a tenuous Spring that would come and go as unpredictably as the changing energies in their house. But when the warmer weather stayed, she dared to hope that each of them would at last find a new direction.

- - -

Along with the passing of the seasons came a distinct change in her moods. Some days felt like new adventure; on other days she could barely move, heavy with her own frustration and impatience. Those were the times when she felt as though she had been set adrift in an endless ocean without a compass or a map. She hoped for guidance, direction, renewal: a wind to blow her raft beyond the choppy waves and into a safe harbor, toward a new awakening, and a renewing of her tired spirit.

The problem and solution exist simultaneously.

The problem was apparent - sometimes. But what was the solution?

Nevertheless, the words struck a nerve, and she held them close to her heart.

- - -

Meanwhile, little things began to go wrong: caught in her

own emotional turmoil, her body was slowly beginning to fall apart.

In the past, she'd been the picture of good health, rarely missing a day at work. Now, however, after nine years with her company, she was scheduled for a second surgery this year. She had used all her sick days for the year for the first one, and would have to start on her vacation time to compensate for the half-pay disability they offered for the second surgery. She felt as though she were fast heading toward the bottom; even getting up in the morning was sometimes major accomplishment.

But once you've hit bottom, the only way to go is back up.

She clung tightly to the words and waited for what was to come.

PART III

FIRE:
PENETRATING THE SHADOWS

We tend to make
the Crossroads confusing

Embracing your Destiny means
rising to meet your challenge
instead of sidestepping your One Mind,
frightened to lift your eyes to the Universe.
Rebirth is dangerous and painful
but can be done with the gracefulness of the swan.
No more waiting.

A sign from our lost nature,
which will fall away like a snake shedding it skin.
Hoping against hope for some kind of sign,
but knowing
the signs are already in place.

See what's real. Heal yourself.
Don't rely on ancient teachings
to save an energy that doesn't die.
It breathes life,
hoping to gain some insight,
hoping to set your balance,
straining to go forward.

Get up. Walk!
Head out as if the path is right in front of you.
Lingering will stagnate your soul,
which is the essence of the Light we all possess,
but cannot remember.
Think about the lost souls whose stubborn egos wouldn't allow
any positive, refreshing Light,
but only dispelling the fear will set you free
and allow you to become
one constant Voice.

She was sitting on "her" rock in the mountains. Though it was midday, the sky seemed darker than usual; had the moon eclipsed the sun? She felt cold from the skin all the way down to her spirit, which seemed to be fading with the waning sunlight.

Just as before, he was standing on a distant rock. Slowly, he turned toward her. Something was different about his eyes, though she didn't know what it was. They were translucent, illuminated by a recognition that came only from the spirit within. His eyes, once pained, were now peaceful, enlightened; they neither saw nor recognized her. She felt that she had ceased to exist to him. But it didn't matter; whatever had created the pain from before had finally been put to rest.

It was evident that, for him, nothing mattered in their collective world anymore. He was now where he needed to be.

She looked at the sky again; the sun was coming out. What she thought was an eclipse, was actually a cloud passing over the sun. She would soon be warm again.

- - -

Was this a dream? she wondered. It was 2:30 a.m.

- - -

Lifestyles of the fast and furious:
We get nowhere in a heartbeat.

Life in itself can be a continuous merry-go-round.

For the majority of us, most of our time is spent earning a living, trying to make ends meet. We may be busy supporting families, building for the future; our lives are hectic, and we're headed everywhere at breakneck speed. We may have spent little time thinking about what we would really like to do with our lives, whether we're happy where we are right now, or where we'd like to be if we are not.

While some of us may be happy in our careers and our lives, still others might have found that our careers, situations or circumstances are not going quite as anticipated. We may be working at jobs where we feel less than satisfied; we may find that we had been giving or taking too little or too much in our relationships, or that our well-laid plans backfired in some way.

For those of us who are not where we would like to be, we continue on with business-as-usual because we aren't certain what we'd like to do, or where we are even going; we may have responsibilities and commitments to maintain, need the money from that dead-end job, despite the mundane tasks and difficult coworkers. Or perhaps we choose to remain in a relationship going nowhere, out of a sense of duty. We simply live out our lives as they unfold.

Regardless of whether our circumstances are benefiting or deterring our happiness, or whether we are doing what we really want to do in life, there comes a time when we do begin to question the circumstances in our lives, even if we are completely happy. For some, it could be a gradual process as subtle as a tide receding at sunset; for others, it could be in a heartbeat. But the questions remain the same, and they are endless: Where am I going? Where should I be, if I'm not supposed to be here, and what should I be doing?

As we have learned, we are becoming aware: we've lost our former complacency and have indeed begun to densensitize. Life is becoming a giant question mark; now we'd like to begin seeking answers.

- - - - -

The key to our Destiny lies in the present.

Ever since the dawn of time, mankind has always pondered the question:

Why are we here?

No one is allowed to tell us why we were put upon this earth, and what each of us was meant to accomplish in our lives. The individual answers must be determined by that person alone, for the answers lie deep within that individual's heart.

The true purpose for our existence on this earth is our destiny: it is the contract into which we entered with the Universe before we were born.

While knowing the nature of one's destiny might seem a mysterious, esoteric concept, in fact, it is not. For some people, it might be directly related to what they are doing now, and they continue on in their paths, fully aware of their goals, and attaining satisfaction along the way.

But for those of us who do not know the nature of our destiny, we would probably want essentially the same thing: we would want to do whatever it is that makes us happy, whether it be in our careers, in our hobbies, or with our families. Hopefully, it would be something that we could do all of the time, a majority of the time, or at least for enough time to make us fully appreciate our existence on this earth.

And of course, we would want to make a positive, beneficial difference to other people and for the world around us, whether it be with a group of people or a solitary activity.

Determining the nature of our destiny is a gradual process: we proceed along our paths, periodically asking the Universe, listening, and then waiting for the answer. It may take some time to hear it, because we may not be ready to know yet. So in the meantime, we must be willing to watch, wait and learn.

If we need to wait awhile to find our answers, we must remember that there are reasons behind the situations in which we find ourselves, regardless of whether we've chosen to be there or not. There might be lessons we need to learn that have nothing to do with the occupation or the situation itself: the Universe is presenting us with the tools we will need to acquire before we progress on our path, and it is a path which we will eventually take, whether we are aware of its existence or not at this time. We may need to develop a stronger character, or we might have to teach others about right action, conscience or fairness. It is up to us to determine the lessons we need to teach and learn, for with every situation, we do both.

Chances are, if we were faced with the "shocking reality" of our true destiny, but we lacked the proper tools to handle it, we could be so overwhelmed by its identity that we would probably run screaming in the opposite direction from it!

So if we find ourselves unable to leave or change our jobs or other situations when we have tried our hardest and desire it most, however, we must remind ourselves that this roadblock is only temporary and won't last forever, regardless of how long it might feel! If we can't figure out where we're supposed to go, then we're not ready to move on. If such is the case, then most important of all the lessons we need to learn is that we need to concentrate on being happy right where we are, right now: we need to learn acceptance. While our circumstances might have been created in a heartbeat, the world was not. Similarly, to extricate ourselves from difficult or uncomfortable circumstances might take more time than we'd like as well.

Sometimes, it is our perspective on a situation that need to be changed before we can progress: we may need the patience to recognize and accept it for what it is, forgive others if necessary, and understand that, for our own betterment, the timing must be conducive for change. While we do have our aspirations, desires and dreams, the Universe knows what we want and need better than we do; we may even be surprised to find that deep down in our subconscious, these were the very same things that our hearts have always wanted.

Often, the most important, yet difficult and continually-learned lesson of all is that of acceptance of the Now, and the willingness to wait for the right time to change. Such are two of the greatest attributes of a Spiritual Warrior.

So, Here is where we need to be, and Now is what we must accept: our lessons are contained in our present situation, regardless of what we might think. Once learned, and when the time is right, then we are ready to move on, and not a moment sooner.

When the time is right, we will know.

- - - - -

Patterns in the now:
A meditation to determine
Our self-limiting behaviors

As warriors of Spirit, each of us has all the attributes which, if they are now underutilized, can be activated to help us to see our way clear in the face of adversity. When we utilize our total harmony of mind-body-spirit, we enable the full use of these attributes. With Spirit as guide, embodied in the protection of the helmet (mind) and shield (body) we find our weapons manifested as intuition, instinct, telepathy and the ability to listen, discern and decide the course of right action with each situation in which we find ourselves.

The following meditation will help to determine the self-limiting attributes and behavioral patterns that hold us back in our spiritual development. While we might be aware of some of them, others might not be as apparent, if they are buried deep within our subconscious mind.

Such limiting traits can range from anger, self-criticism, or criticism of others, helping others when they haven't sought our assistance, or repeatedly helping someone with the same problem when they did seek our assistance (both acts would deprive others of responsibilities they themselves alone should assume). Others might involve guilt, inferiority, fear or a lack of courage; perhaps we seek control of others by manipulating them for our own personal gain. Other issues might involve integrity, such as habitual lying; some might be related to a lack of confidence or self-esteem, inappropriate (compulsive) substance use or abuse (any kind of activity used as a distraction or escape). Yet others might involve spiritual pride or the perspective that there is only one right way to perform a task.

When we are willing to recognize their existence, we have taken the first step toward spiritual progression, and for this we are to be commended. To begin the journey, we must take the first step.

- - - - -

As with all the meditations, it is more effective if you sit in a chair or on the floor, keeping your spine erect.

Begin by breathing deeply, inhaling the positive and exhaling the negative.

Once you are calm, focused and centered, visualize the White Light above you. Feel it shining, then penetrating the top of your head, down through your spine, outward through your body and all around you, completely surrounding you. Gradually relax each part of your body as the Light moves along your spine.

As you continue breathing, feel your breath moving throughout your body.

Think back over the past 24 hours. What did you do? Did you go to work? School? Was it your day off?

How did you spend your time? Did you interact with a lot of people, or did you spend your time alone? Was it by choice or circumstance? Did you feel happy, sad, uneasy, peaceful, or something else, or a combination of many feelings? Were you restless or did you feel the need to do something, but didn't know what to do?

If you were at work, were you caught in a difficult situation with a coworker? Did you perform your routine duties? Were you given an award or recognition for a "job well done"? If you were at home, did you do some gardening, relax, enjoy the day? Go shopping?

Now, think back to the events over the past week, and focus especially on your feelings surrounding each one. Did you have a positive week? Or was it difficult or challenging? What are your reactions to the events that now come to mind?

If you seek more insight into the "big picture," think back over the past month, several months or even the past year, contemplating the events which first come to mind. Regardless of their seeming insignificance, you remembered them first for a reason, and that alone is special cause for their consideration.

If nothing important seems to be coming out of this exercise, consider your actions or feelings surrounding a recent event or two. For example, did you cancel an upcoming visit with a difficult relative because you weren't feeling well? Perhaps your sub-conscious was protecting you from the confrontations you consis-tently face when battling this individual over old, well-covered ground, and your physical was reacting as a means of self-preser-vation. This might be an example of finding the courage to stand up for your own convictions and demand respect for yourself, as well as your opinions: Spirit needs to come forth in a positive way, rather than Mind creating a negative reaction, manifested in the Physical self.

If you received recognition or a raise for a job well done at work, yet felt empty nevertheless, consider the reasons behind your emptiness. Did feel that you weren't worthy of that raise? Perhaps you felt pressured to exceed the performance the next time? Did you feel guilty because you were taught long ago that to feel pride or satisfaction is "wrong"? Did you feel bad because you felt that somebody else should have received a raise as well? Did you feel empty because you felt that you are now making lots of money, but are unsatisfied with your job and now you feel that you have to stay because there is no "logical" reason to leave?

Continue to breathe deeply for a few more minutes, gently focusing on the White Light in and around you as you inhale and exhale. When you are ready, gradually open your eyes, feeling refreshed and lighter.

And, as you continue your activities for the day, remember that the Light is always around you, and that with each breath, you are inhale the protective White Light.

- - - - -

When you are ready, journal your thoughts, feelings and impressions surrounding the events that you contemplated. Again, it is important to note which events first came to mind, for those were the most significant to you. Be honest in your answers; no one need read them except yourself.

Our behaviors and feelings behind the events that occur in our lives serve us a purpose of sorts. What do think they do? What do you wish they did? When you answer these questions, consider yet another one: Are they appropriate to who we are now?

If you feel uncomfortable about any of the thoughts or feelings you noted, consider that also. Your subconscious might be telling you something of which you may not already be aware, or do not want to face.

Always remember that, if you are uncomfortable about any behavior or pattern, it is your free will and choice whether you decide to change it or not. Whatever your decision, however, remember that, from the Divine perspective, it is already changed. We came into this world open, innocent and free; once we have left, we will be the same way, just as we will always be so throughout eternity. The only issue lies in the challenge of the everyday mind, manifested in the Now: Will we rise to that challenge so that we are consciously aware of this wholeness in this lifetime?

How long it takes is up to us .

- - - - -

Focus is the key, but it's not an issue.

Having determined our limiting behavioral patterns, we are better able to handle the various difficulties which might arise. It is important to remember the are pitfalls and that we must always maintain our full awareness by paying attention, as the road might sometimes become arduous and exhausting.

To do so requires focus or concentration.

But when our skills are second nature to us, we can apply them easily, and reenergize ourselves in the process. When we focus our skills, they become our tools, and from them, we attain our power. We then apply our power to the task at hand. It is the task itself, then, that becomes the issue, and not the attainment of the skills needed to complete it.

- - - - -

The tighter we cling, the harder it is to let go.

I will heal their backsliding, I will love them freely;
for mine anger is turned away from him.
- Hosea 14:4

Once we have decided that we would like to embark on our own personal path toward inner peace, we might find ourselves subconsciously holding on to our self-defeating emotions, habits and behaviors even tighter than before, despite all our best intents and efforts to release them!

Releasing any old, unwanted practices of any type might be difficult for a variety of reasons. If they have served us for a long time, they become like old friends, even if they are ultimately damaging to ourselves (and/or possibly to others as well), and for that reason alone it is difficult to release them.

What would we do without them?

We might have to look at things we really don't want to see.

We would have to face our issues, confront the who we are now, and the who we want to be. We would have to redefine ourselves, our values, our goals. We would have to reassess our lives and what we have done with them, and what we would like to do with them now. We might have to endure a lot of heartache, resulting in a lot of pain we may not want to endure. We would have to let go of a lot of baggage, the "stuff" to which we have long been clinging.

We would grieve.

We would have to let go of all that was, for all that was, is no longer appropriate to who we are now: we would have to rebirth.

When we are awakened, enlightened, and seek a better path than the one from which we have come, sometimes we need to bid the old "friends" goodbye, if they are no longer appropriate to who we are becoming.

But time continually passes, and with it also passes the pain, fear, emptiness and all the other inhibiting emotions we might feel during our reassessment process.

And with that passing comes a new sense of inner peace.

- - - - -

Winds of change hasten
rustling, dusk-laden leaves
clouds like shadows glide.

- - - - -

The passage of seasons brought a cool wet, Spring, one that seemed to linger longer than it normally had in the past. She'd never seen one like this before, for there were days when temperatures were cool or even cold, and when it rained, it felt as though it would continue as if the earth were weeping, mourning whatever events that were to come. But then there were the days when the sun would shine and the temperatures would reach the eighty-degree mark. The entire world relaxed and smiled on all its inhabitants, and it seemed that everything would be all right.

Gradually, Spring passed into a sultry, humid Summer, and she hoped that it would be, for the both of them, a time of transformation.

- - -

Despite the heat and humidity, Summer had always been her favorite season. When she was young, it meant that school was out for the year, and it was time to go swimming, vacationing, camping. It was also the time when her birthday would come, and after they were together, late Summer would be the time for his birthday as well. Things seemed to be a little different this Summer, however, for each of them continued to change and grow in opposite directions, and with the changes came the inevitable myriad of interactions and revelations. They began when each attained a different level of sobriety.

His began when, one Saturday, he stopped drinking heavily. It happened overnight: a caring friend made one comment, and it struck a nerve within him. Magically, he stopped, and that was that.

At first, she was confused: Why was he doing this now? she wondered.   Over the years, she wondered if he knew what he was doing to his body, though she said little about it. She had once, but it had little effect on him, if it had any at all. But his behavior hadn't changed, and he continued on as before.

And then she became frightened when she realized that she could no longer hide from him; he might see that she was changing and might begin to question her activities. It was as though someone had lifted a curtain, and she was still standing behind it, as though she should have already left, but didn't know where to go or even what to do. But her fears were quickly put to rest: although he did pay closer attention to her and he did question her activities, he still kept a respectful distance and allowed her to continue as before. And he kept on with his own activities, pleased and relieved that his friends still treated him as they always had, and he was still accepted right along with his new sobriety.

- - -

Finally, she was curious about the ease with which he had stopped drinking. She wondered why changes were so difficult for her, yet seemingly easy for him. Here was a man that was capable of moving the world when he put his mind to it, she thought. Or maybe there was more to it than just that? At any rate, she wanted to know.

Don't you miss the beer? she asked him one day, somewhat afraid to bring it up because she didn't know how he'd react to such a question, yet she was still curious enough to inquire anyway.

A little, he admitted, although pragmatically, and returned to his activity of the moment. Evidently, he had nothing to tell her. She let the matter drop.

And so they continued on together, seemingly in sync, but at a safe distance from each other, and arguing only every once in awhile. For despite the smooth spots, there still remained an undercurrent of dissonance that could not yet be clearly defined. There was something she felt she was missing about the situation.

Stopping the implosion: Beginning to let go.

Coming out of denial, we are not honest by nature.
This is why we continue to return to the Earth.

There comes a time in our spiritual progression when our consciousness has been enlightened, but we somehow remain stuck where we are, blocked on our path and unable to progress toward our destiny. Slowly, we struggle forward, yet many times, we keep pulling ourselves back. It's as though we are trying to walk with our shoelaces tied together!

Subconsciously, we may remain self-imposed prisoners, forcing ourselves to re- live old, past events, resulting in useless emotions and perhaps old, self-defeating behaviors which have long ago served their purpose. Yet even if these behaviors are no longer appropriate, we might still fear taking the first steps toward freedom. Our intuition might be telling us that we must now take a closer look at our existing habits, behaviors and actions and determine what now holds us back.

If we find that our actions have indeed become self-defeating, harmful or negative in some way, we will need to reassess our lives and our present consciousness, for we may have unwittingly lost pieces and fragments of ourselves somewhere along the way. We cannot progress unless we have the totality of ourselves for the journey.

Once we realize the nature of our difficulties, we make the first step toward reclaiming the power and total harmony that was initially our birthright.

If we have become aware that the time to reclaim ourselves, and to right the wrongs in our lives, is Now, then we must currently possess what we need, to tackle the problem. The Universe is simply showing us that the time is right.

- - - - -

The following series of meditations will help us to assess where we presently stand on our path, along with an understanding of the events which brought us to our present consciousness.

First, we will contact our Angels, sometimes known as guides, or spirit guides. These entities, which were assigned to us before our birth, will assist us when we enlist their help and when they are allowed to do so. Two of the many things they are allowed to do are detailed in the following pages: First, they will help us define our goals, and second, they will assist us in seeking a greater insight into the issues that inhibit our spiritual progress.

Our guides will also help us realize that we were not meant to remain alone forever, regardless of our present circumstances. There is indeed someone else out there for us, whether they be soul mates or soul partners. But it could be that we must resolve and transcend the obstacles before us right now, before we can move toward them. As with everything else that happens in our lives, we will meet them, but only when the time and circumstances are right, and when we are ready for their presence in our lives.

- - - - -

Smiling, wit, but no peace
lest I stand alone.
Conviction, courage:
all these things
my own heart needs.

Angels help,
unseen hands make a path for me.
Living out the best that's hiding

> *there*
> *for now all these things I see.*
> *No more stress, worries gone,*
> *fright has no place here.*

> *Thank you for the path I found,*
> *stepping out*
> *in faith, not fear!!!*

Angels: Within us, and around us, helping us along our path

There are many Angels within, and around us. Some may prefer to call them Guardian Angels; others simply prefer the name, Angels, or Guides. Regardless of their name by which we choose to recognize them, however, they are here to help, guide and comfort us as we travel along our path. Depending upon our life's goals (we agreed to the terms of our contract with the Universe, before we were born), we might have several different Angels, or perhaps only one will remain with us throughout our lives. All the duties of our Angels relate to helping us on our journey toward the attainment of total harmony, both with ourselves and by helping others. They are with us always, observing our actions, whether we are alone or around other people. They listen to the thoughts that run through our heads, and help us discern whether our thoughts help or harm us.

As our protectors, our guides not only show us when our thoughts are self-defeating, but they can push us out of harm's way in the face of danger when we are not meant to face it, but have unwittingly been caught in the wrong place at the wrong time.

As our advisors, and when allowed to do so, they assist us in choosing the right path to follow, provided we ask for their help and are willing to listen for the answers. And sometimes, in the Divine Order of things, they must push us onto the appropriate path, whether we like or not: There are times when we might not want to be dragged down the right road, but that's where we might need to be!

Our guides, however, are not allowed to assume our responsibilities that fall upon us, for those are ours alone to assume. This means that they cannot complete a task if we are supposed to do it. The most they can do is advise us on what needs to be done; it is then up to us to take the time, make the effort and do it ourselves. If we did not, we would deprive ourselves of the lessons we need to learn in order to progress. Hence, they give us the little flashes of intuition that lend insight into a difficult problem or issue, and then step back, allowing us to decide what the appropriate plan of action might be.

In many cases, working with our Angels may prove to be a symbiotic relationship. Their own task might be to help us attain one certain goal, and then they might be gone, depending upon the terms of their own contract with the Universe.

This is a learning planet, so when we can fully appreciate the nature and purposes of our guides, we are better able to learn and understand the lessons they attempt to teach us. All of us, as connected one with another, need some help along the way. We might feel satisfied, that, as we learn our lessons and help ourselves and each other, we can also help our guides as much as they can help us.

- - - - -

No longer am I chained
to the lower self,
but asking for a Divine intervention,
knowing I can reach toward,
and count on
the Angels,

unseen by human eyes,
but I am most aware of their presence.

Protect me from the evil of this world,
holding my spirit to touch
the face of the Universe within and
without.
Pleased to know my soul is quiet,
because the Plan is already in place,
and trusting that I will follow,
listening
to all myself, for the answers that I have
already known
down through the ages,
holding firm to my convictions,
knowing that all is well.

Contacting our angels:
A meditation

The following meditation will help us contact our Angels or guides. (The terms, Angels, guides or spirit guides will be used interchangeably throughout these meditations.) This guide (or guides, if you have more than one), will assist you with the following exercises.

When we contact our guides, we enlist the help of those more powerful and knowledgeable than ourselves, for through them, we call upon the power of the Universe, good and true. And through this experience, we can be satisfied that we become strengthened and enriched through the process.

- - - - -

Begin by breathing deeply, inhaling the positive and exhaling the negative. While you are breathing, find the White Light shining above you, warm, safe and comforting. Feel any stresses or problems gradually melting and falling away from you, gradually dissolving on the floor around you and disappearing, while the White Light ever strengthens you, penetrating to your heart, illuminating your skin, hair and body. Feel this energy from the White Light, as it further strengthens you and finally begins to sustain you. See the glow reflected on the outer surface of your body and close in around you.

When you are ready and feel confident and strong from the energies of the White Light, turn around and find the golden door in front of you. Carefully notice it: Is it round, rectangular? Does it have a shiny brass knob, or does the door have some other fixture for a knob, such as a brass ring?

Open the door, and walk through it. Walk up the flight of stairs and into the field beyond.

The field beyond the golden door is a peaceful place. This is a place of Nature, the place where you are most comfortable, whether it be a green, grassy meadow, an aromatic pine forest, or a flat, sandy beach with a jade-green ocean. Remember, too, that this is the peaceful place which enables you to attune with your Higher Self, your intuition which unites all souls as One. This is also the place where all the answers come, those which are true, good and from the Universe.

Look carefully around you. What do you see?

Carefully note the details of your surroundings. Are the colors intense, or pastel shades? Is the sun shining brightly? Do you see birds overhead? Are there animals hiding in the bushes close by? See how many details you can spot, even the little ones. Take time to do this; this is your time, a time of love, peace and learning.

As you look around you, continue to breathe deeply in and out. This will continue to balance, center, focus and stabilize you.

Look around again, this time for any human forms. See who comes into your field, or who was there all along, but not visible to you previously. When you see another spirit, carefully note his or her appearance.

Always, there are two attributes that your Angel must have. First, he or she must be of a Higher Form, that is, one good, true and from the Universe. To determine this, ask the question aloud: "Are you true, good and from the Universe?"

Now, listen carefully for the answer. Any answer other than an immediate and definitive Yes! is unacceptable. If you do not immediately hear this, then tell that spirit to get out of your space, and it will disappear.

Secondly, look at the spirit's eyes. Are they straight? If they are not straight and kind, again tell it to get out of your space. Always remember that, whether you are in the field or even in the everyday world, the eyes of another will tell you what you need to know about them, for the eyes are indeed the windows of the soul.

If the spirit before you has not told you that it is good, true and from the Universe, or it does not have straight, kind eyes, then banish it from your field. Any spirit lacking these two attributes denotes a spirit of a lower form; such a spirit is incapable of teaching the lessons you need to progress on your path. Most importantly, however, trust your intuition. When you have attained clarity, you can sense what is right for you. Hence, if you feel uncomfortable about the spirit before you, tell it to leave.

When you are satisfied with the appearance and energies of your guide and feel completely comfortable with it, you may ask your guide anything you wish.

Always remember, however, to begin your question or request with the phrase, "In the Divine Order of things. . ." for your answers to be from the Highest nature. Make certain that your requests and questions are clearly and simply stated. Although your guides are of the highest Intelligence, clear communication is essential. Just as with all energies, we receive back what we send out. If a question is unclear, the answer may return just as convoluted as it was initially sent.

Communicate freely with your guide. You may have a running conversation with him or her, or you may simply prefer to listen to the answer. Perhaps you need a sounding board, someone to hear you out on an issue, as you might prefer to simply talk your way through a problem or difficult challenge. Your guide is always there for you, and does not pass any judgments whatsoever. He or she will help you with your observations and assist you to strengthen and utilize your intuition.

When you have completed your conversation with your guide, thank him or her for the wisdom imparted to you, or for the sympathetic listening ear, and bid farewell. Always remember to be courteous and kind; we would expect no less from them.

At this time, you may leave the field by descending the stairs which initially led you here. Find the golden door; open it, and walk through it to your present place. Close it firmly behind you. Always remember to close it behind you when you return.

At your own pace, open your eyes, coming out of the meditation with the wisdom that has been imparted to you by your guide. You are now ready to go about your daily activities in a positive, constructive manner, feeling enriched and satisfied that you have contacted and attuned with your guide from the Higher Self.

- - - - -

Preparing for the Journey:
A word about change.

For centuries, man has long realized that the only constant in the human experience is change. Everything on earth and in the Universe, regardless of what it might be, undergoes a transformation of sorts, whether it be quick or slow, natural or as a result of forced intervention by mankind.

Change can be either easy or difficult to accept at times, depending upon our perspective and willingness to adapt and learn from the change, as well as the energy and value we place upon it. If we perceive a change as positive, and transmit a positive energy upon it, we are more willing to adapt to it; if we view it as negative, we impose negative energies upon it. Hence, the change then becomes a difficult challenge.

Regardless of our perception of any specific change as either positive or negative, and regardless of how easily we adapt to it, however, change, in its teaching capacity, always provides us with an opportunity for spiritual growth.

Similarly, as the passage of time facilitates changes, time also facilitates our opportunities for spiritual growth. As with time, then, our awareness and willingness to adapt to change becomes not only necessary, but evolutionary as well: change is the natural order of things, and as humans with One Soul, all of us are progressing toward the Light. The only variable factor becomes the amount of time we take to reach it.

As we work with the succeeding meditations, visualizations and exercises, and begin to modify our existing habits and behavioral patterns, we become more aware of the purposes behind our activities and the emotions that had generated the activities. For awhile, we are caught up in the activity of change itself, for the activity requires an adjustment period as we assimilate new, positive activities, emotions and attitudes.

Experts have indicated that changing a habit usually requires a period of twenty-one days. However, depending upon the person and the activity itself, the time required for the change might be shorter or longer.

Regardless of the amount of time needed for anyone to implement change, however, once the novelty of new activities surrounding the resulting change has worn off, the satisfaction of the accomplishment with victory over the old habits lessens. For some, the new, positive behaviors might become as mundane as yet another habit. We might feel that we are lacking something, that something is missing, yet we cannot specifically identify it.

We may become lost again, if we are not prepared for this period. At this point, we simply remind ourselves that we must be prepared to live empty for a time. What was once full must be emptied for the ultimate progression to occur.

- - - - -

Understanding and accepting void and emptiness in our lives

There are two types of feelings surrounding the lack resulting from the assimilation of a positive change: void and emptiness. When we begin to feel either one, we need to be reminded that there are differences between the two: void, when considered as a perspective based upon human consciousness, connotes an awareness of a loss, whereas emptiness, as part of the natural order of things, is simply a state of being. Emptiness, then, can also be defined as a time of rest before regeneration.

Despite our realization that we need to endure the void or emptiness, there may be times when we become tired of the seemingly endless lack. We might even feel that this period might last forever. When or if this does occur, we need to remind ourselves that this consciousness is only temporary, that we must have faith that the better times will come, and that patience is needed to await the passage of time and the proper circumstances before new and positive things begin to occur.

All must be ready and in place at the Divine right time before any regeneration process occurs. If we aren't ready for a period of new growth, we may be ill-equipped to handle the responsibilities and commitment that might be required of us. During these times, then, we remember that the very same time period we might consider as an eternity, to the Universe is a merely the blink of an eye.

- - - - -

Understanding Universal time:
A visualization

We can perceive time as passing quickly when we concentrate, and focus on the task at hand. We realize that we need to go about our business in a positive, productive manner, regardless of our perspective in the Now.

But we can also remember that there is a distinction between chronological time and Universal time: while chronological time is important as we go about the tasks of the day, the events in our lives occur as ordered by Universal time.

Understanding concept of time as expressed by both aspects, and knowing the importance of chronological time in our daily lives, then, we might need to be reminded of the manner in which Universal time passes. The following visualization will assist us in doing just that.

- - - - -

As always, we begin by breathing deeply, inhaling the positive, and exhaling the negative. Periodically, we remind ourselves that Time is a concept relative to each of us, and that an appreciation of both Universal time and patience are required for spiritual wholeness.

As we continue breathing, we clear any stresses and problems as well as balancing, focusing and centering ourselves. Surround yourself in the White Light; feel its warmth and strong, positive energies encircling you and radiating from within. As you feel this, realize that you are becoming stronger and stronger, that its tranquil rays render you impervious to any negativity from within or without.

Imagine that you are floating effortlessly above the earth, surrounded by the White Light. The atmosphere is dark, the color is nondescript. Off in the distance is the earth; from this angle, it is a deep, navy blue.

As you view the earth, you notice that it is encompassed by long, wispy white clouds, which intermittently change their shapes, depending upon the wind currents and rotational forces emanating from the earth itself. Sometimes the clouds change direction, sometimes they barely seem to move at all. Yet the earth continually rotates, albeit ever so slowly. Sometimes it is even difficult to see the earth rotating; you must focus upon one spot in the land mass to see this rotation.

Yet as you carefully watch, you feel assured that, despite its seeming leisurely movement, the earth does continue to move. Changes are occurring; from this vantage point, it is easy to understand the magnitude of each change as it directly and sometimes indirectly affects other people and other things.

We can be further assured that whatever void or emptiness we feel inside, however painful or overwhelmingly vast it might now feel, will pass with time, and with this passage of time, the pain will be replaced by another feeling, one that is better than the feeling that initially preceded the feeling of lack. We remind ourselves that any pain we feel at the present time is only an everyday, mind-based perception, that this is a time of rest and gestation before a regeneration, renewal and replacement of the lesser with the greater...

- - - - -

When you are ready, slowly return to your surroundings. Contemplate the world around you; remember that indeed, situations and circumstances can, and do change, with the blink of the Universal eye. . .

- - - - -

The work: A series of Meditations:

*Assessing the circumstances
from the beginning.*

- - - - -

The following meditations will help us identify some of the troublesome issues which might impede our progress and influence our negative behavioral patterns. They will also help us to determine what keeps us mired in the old ways. As with many of the other meditations and visualizations, keep some paper and a pen or pencil close by; you will come to some interesting realizations during these exercises.

Since the process can be quite involved and time-consuming, it is advisable to complete one section of questions at a time, and then take a break. Or, if you prefer, simply read the questions first, contemplate them, and then answer them. Whichever method you choose, however, listen to your intuition, as this will determine your best plan of action.

Regardless of the method by which you answer these questions, it is essential that you meditate and work with your Angels, guide or guides, for the most complete and enlightening answers.

- - - - -

As we remember, this meditation, as well as all the others, is more effective if you sit, either in a chair, or on the floor, with your spine erect.   Begin by breathing deeply, remembering to focus on your breathing patterns throughout the meditation, inhaling the positive energies and exhaling the negative influences that impede your spiritual progression.

Once you are completely calm, focused and centered, and you feel the White Light above you, shining through your body and all around you. When it has completely covered you with its warm, comforting Light, gradually relax each part of your body. Call upon your Angel or Angels for guidance; you know that they will help you determine the nature and extent of the issues that inhibit your progress.

Then, when you are fully calm and relaxed and your Angels are with you, begin to drift backward in time...

Begin your assessment by contemplating your childhood, and then answer the following questions. These questions were designed to specifically identify the birth or childhood conditions that cause you to be the way you are today:

* First, select an event in your childhood which you know influences your behavior in some way, at this time in your life. It could be your earliest memory, your happiest one or even one that is painful.
  What was the event?

* Contemplate this event in detail, and then describe it. Begin by remembering the objects that surrounded you. What were the colors of these objects? What were their textures? What sounds did you hear?

* How did you feel about this event at that time? Were you happy, sad? Excited, fearful? If this memory was painful for you, why was it painful? What made it significant for you? How does this recollection influence you today?

* Do you have children? In answering this question, did this memory in some way influence you from either having, or not having any children? If you do have children of your own, did this memory consciously or subconsciously influence you to either make sure that your own children had a similar memory, if the memory was pleasant, or if it was painful, was this an experience one which you would prefer that they avoid altogether?

* Next, contemplate a childhood event which particularly stands out in your mind, regardless of whether or not you

know it influences your present behavior. Following the procedure above, answer the same questions.

Take the time and jot down your answers. When you are satisfied with your answers, that they are as complete and as honest as possible, and put them aside if you desire.
When you are ready, continue with the next section.

- - - - -

In the now:
The ego defined

For this next exercise, as with all the others, we begin by breathing and surrounding ourselves in the White Light. Then, find your Angels. . .

* When you are fully comfortable and relaxed, contemplate the situations and events that you now face in your daily life. How are they influencing your habits? What is the immediate impact they have on your lifestyle?
  After you have completed these events, answer the following:

* What is the one thing you have long denied yourself in your life?
  This relates to something of a non-material nature, such as staying calm in a challenging situation, or the ability to stand up for yourself when you need to. Perhaps it might be that you feel guilty, when you are feeling happy, and the others around you choose not share in your happiness.

* Then, name something in which you pride yourself, something you have which is not possessed by everyone else. What is it about this attribute that sets you apart from others? If everyone else had the same attribute, how would you feel? Be honest with yourself, even if the answers may not be ones

of which you are particularly proud. No one else except yourself need see these answers. They are not meant to be degrading or demeaning; rather, they are meant to enlighten you.

Remember, the first step toward spiritual progression is honesty to yourself.

- - - - -

When you are ready, continue with the following questions:

* Describe an incident in your life, where your ego cost you something. It could be anything, from a missed opportunity, a failure of sorts, or an event in which you may have confronted someone in a manner you later came to regret.

  Begin by describing the situation itself and the nature of the challenge. What did you do, or what did you have to do? Did you have to the sacrifice something for the desired situation to come about? Did it happen?

- What is your perception between the illusion (how you perceived the situation) and the reality (of what really was)?
- If you had to do it over again, what would you do now?
- How would you see the situation, had you done it differently?

In answering this question, consider the role your ego played, and consider the positive uses of adversity in the situation. A good example would be that anger can be cleansing, if used as an impetus to resolve the challenge, rather than limiting, if we remain lost in the negative aspect of the emotion.

- - - - -

Through crisis, we grow

Many times, we face a challenge or crisis in our lives which, when it is over, leaves us permanently changed in some way. Although the incidents themselves might not be avoidable, the

manner in which we perceive and ultimately handle the circumstances within and surrounding them, can be changed.

Sometimes the greatest lessons we learn and the ones most-
often remembered, are those where either the situations or the
circumstances surrounding them were most painful. Much can
be learned about ourselves; intuitively we can learn and appreciate first-hand, the difference between impressions and judgements.

- - - - -

Impressions and Judgments:
A meditation

Impressions and judgements continually pervade our mind.
In our daily existence, we observe others around us and and the
circumstances in which we find ourselves. We continually
receive impressions or make judgements; consciously or unconsciously, we decide whether they serve us some purpose, and
then either dismiss, or act upon the information as we deem
appropriate.

As we have probably already realized, impressions come
from our subconscious mind, whereas judgments come from our
everyday, reasoning mind, shaded and filtered by own personal
perspectives, likes and dislikes.

Judgements can be valid when we are able to impartially
assess an individual's actions and determine the true contents of
their heart. Yet judgements can also impair our capacity to form
clear impressions when we allow them to dominate our thinking,
and use them as our sole input for the actions of another or the
outward appearances of any given situation.

Knowing the difference between judgements and impressions
and their place in our spiritual development, we need to pay
close attention to both, and be able to distinguish the difference
between the two as we form both. When we are clear and free of
our own issues and better attuned to our instincts, this task will

become easier through time and awareness.

During the following meditation, contemplate the distinction between impressions and judgements. . .

* Before going into meditation, think of a situation in your life where you were experiencing a pivotal point or crisis that needed clearing:

First, summarize the situation. What was the crisis that changed your life?

Next, determine the challenge you faced, along with the course of action you decided upon, including any sacrifices you had to make in order to clear the troublesome issues.

Finally, determine what exactly the evolved situation was, when all was said and done.

* When you have done this, go into meditation and get in touch with the Higher Self; contact your Angel and Angels. . .

Now, give the same overview after the meditation. (When you do so, you step outside yourself and view the situation from a Higher perspective. In other words, you see it, and then hop the fence!)

Remember that there is a difference between intuition and mental reasoning. Mental reasoning are the thoughts we create as a result of the everyday mind, the "What-would-the-average-person-do-in-this-situation" problem-solving mode that many of us assume, when we attempt to determine a solution to our problems. When we use our intuition, however, we clear our mind of any unwanted negative, inhibiting thoughts, enabling the voice of the Higher Self to filter through. We determine the best possible solution for everyone involved, regardless of the sacrifice.

Again, when you are ready, come out of the meditation and jot down your answers. Rest before you begin the next section.

Dissolving the fear

As with many other self-limiting emotions, fear is a powerful energy, for it can be quickly transmitted to any group of people and spread like wildfire. Since we have been taught to be fearful from a very early age, this probably is one reason why people so easily and immediately feel fear: highly receptive in our youth, we have learned our lessons well. And since humans are inherently telepathic, fear is thus easily transmitted and received. All of us can identify fear when we feel it.

But when we harness that fear by pausing for a few moments, stepping back and assessing it, we can identify the type of fear with which we are faced. We can then allow ourselves to constructively react, and tackle the problem at hand. When we pause and listen to the One clear Voice of the intuition, we can allow ourselves to catch our breath and arrest the negative, energy-wasting, self-destructive activities.

As we may have learned earlier, there are two types of fear: instinctive and reasoning. Instinctive fear is that which is immediately felt in a survival situation. For example, if we see a threatening situation, we fear for our survival. Once that threat is acknowledged, we can put our fears to one side and decide upon a plan of action and then execute it, thereby allowing ourselves a greater chance of survival.

Reasoning fear is the type upon which we brood: it is the product of the everyday reasoning mind. We do not see any immediate threat, but we allow the hypothetical scenarios to become the monsters in our head, refusing to allow the What if this happened? or What do I do if...? to rest.

Planning ahead is a good idea, for if, or when we are faced with the situation, we know what to do. But to worry about something after we have planned for any possible alternatives serves no purpose, except to generate more worry and internal disharmony. As with any factor that limits our spiritual progress, then, reasoning fear must be eliminated, for it inhibits our intuition and spiritual growth as well as our opportunities for constructive action.

- - - -

Transcending guilt and fear

Guilt is another self-limiting emotion that we must seek to eliminate after it has served its purpose. Guilt, when understood as a sense of conscience we place upon ourselves, is healthy when constructively used to enable a sense of courtesy and responsibility toward others: through constructive guilt, we seek atonement or correction of the perceived wrongdoing, and in the process, we learn a better way to act for the future. But an exaggerated sense of guilt limits our progression when we have done what we could to correct the situation, but are not releasing either the issue or the guilt itself.

Fear and guilt can be closely related to one another: when we seek to release either one or the other, the one upon which we do not focus will appear as a reason that we cannot let the other go. In either case, the results are the same: our progression is blocked; we might somehow believe that we do not deserve to be free of either guilt or fear.

When we seek to eliminate guilt, then, we might become fearful of taking that first step, perhaps believing that we do not deserve to be free. Similarly, when we seek to eradicate fear, we might feel guilty for wanting to do so, again believing that we do not deserve to change. We can probably say, then, that to eliminate any one emotion can initiate the onset of the other.

Working to effect a change of any type can be an unsettling process. We are pushing ourselves out into the sunlight, away from the security of that darkened movie theater, and into an unknown and possibly unfriendly environment. The process can be quite painful and uncomfortable for awhile.

If we need to stay in the theater for that same old movie because we are frightened of the change, then this is where we need to be. When we're ready, we'll peek out again. But when we don't want to stay inside anymore and want to change, then we must step out in faith: our intuition is telling us that it is time, that we are ready to take that first step out into the light, as difficult as it might feel. And whether we seek first to change either guilt or fear, we must realize that the other will probably be following on its heels as a defense mechanism to keep our behavior unchanged, attempting to drive us back into the shadows for the late show rerun. But we have to push beyond the fear and the negative, self-limiting energy, and just do it.

For awhile, we will be unsteady, unsure, perhaps wondering if we have done the right thing by trying to change. But we remember that we might encounter the pain of void and emptiness while attempting to change. Yet we must also remember that the energy we put into our efforts will eventually return to us: when we are confident that we can, and will change, that we are perceiving correctly, and that these feelings of uncertainty are temporary, then they too, will pass, allowing the new, positive, confident energies to shine through.

- - - - -

Dissolving and transcending:
Releasing guilt and fear

As we have done with all the others, we begin this 20-minute meditation by breathing and surrounding ourselves in the White Light.

Then, finding our Angels, contemplate the following. . .

* List three things of which you are frightened today, starting with situations and circumstances. They could be people, certain places, certain situations. For example, do you fear speaking in public? High places?

* Then, list three people who are troublesome when you must deal with them.

* Finally, name three fears that you're ready to release, something you felt that you needed to possess, regardless of the cost or consequences, and something you know deep down in your heart, limits your spiritual progress. Such fears could be a need to control the ones you love because you are afraid of being alone, a fear of illness, even when you're rarely sick, or a need to help a friend, even when he or she didn't ask for it, but you feel that you know what they need anyway.
As you contemplate these questions more fully, ask your

79

Angel or Angels more about the specific nature of these fears, and why you have these.

When you are satisfied with your answers and conversations, return to the everyday world, and write down everything that happened: what you learned, what you saw, what was discussed. To complete these questions, write three paragraphs describing each of the answers, along with three ways to resolve the challenging situation.

* In considering the responses to the above exercise, if you could heal one thing in your life, what would it be?

When you feel that you have the answers you need, or at least have raised your awareness of any self-limiting traits driven out of fear, come slowly out of this meditation. Take a few days, if necessary, to think about, and ponder the answers you found to these questions. As with all these meditations, it may take awhile to fully complete this assignment, for all of us are complicated human beings with many sub-issues lodged and hidden within, and behind the main issues.

As you may have expected, these meditations were designed to initiate and perpetuate a healing process, for healing in and of itself is of an evolutionary nature, just as was mankind's physical progression. Remember, we did not come into our present mindset overnight; similarly, to permanently or profoundly heal any difficulties created by the ego-driven, everyday reasoning mind will not be an overnight process either. All we need are faith, belief and willingness to change, for when we possess the willingness and active affirm it, it will become our reality.

– – – – –

We don't need an asylum, We need a wake-up call!

As we send out positive energies into the world, we find that we begin to receive them back, for what we send out, we receive.

We become more confident in our spiritual abilities, manifested into our new and greater Reality; we have begun to learn and appreciate the significance of our lessons. Our path of becomes a smoother one, one of a more consistent progression. We are more capable of, at the very least, recognizing, or better yet, learning or altogether resolving our challenges and difficult situations. We are better able to handle the obstacles that cast the shadows of doubt across our path, and now do so with greater clarity, aware-ness and inner peace; we begin to relax. Our world is, for us, a better, happier and more peaceful place.

We may look back upon our early attempts at advancement and decide that the difficulties we'd initially faced are behind us, that our problems are no longer issues. We begin to doubt their existence in the first place, that this troubled perspective was all an illusion. What did we see, and what did we really think we saw?

Perhaps we were the Givers all along, that we never had assumed the role of a Taker. Perhaps this was a result of our flawed thinking, dissipated by our greater awareness and under-standing.

In the face of this pending Return To Complacency, we might get a few minor jolts from the Universe: irritating situations might begin to recur. Perhaps that noisy and judgmental relative invited us for a visit, rehashing the old issues that were raised before; some new coworkers might have been introduced into our company, ones that have an even harder-line stance than the previous ones who left.

While the reasons behind some of these events might be root-ed in old karmic issues (covered in a later chapter), it is not important to determine now whether this is the reason for the difficulty. What is more important is to remember that the Universe is giving us a wake-up call.

When we get a wake-up call of sorts, we realize that we are still on the path, that we can handle this. We have advanced to the point of awareness by shedding the initial complacency that had imprisoned us. We also realize that every so often, the Universe gives us a test, a "reality check," so that we can assure ourselves that we are better able to handle these challenges. Although seeing the same issues arise might be frustrating, we can now handle them with a greater ease, since we have been down this path before.

- - - - -

Rising to the Challenge
means we have to get up

As our power increases, so also does the magnitude of our responsibilities.

When we advance spiritually, we demonstrate to the Universe that we are willing to change by rising above our ego. We do so as best we can by recognizing our mistakes and short-comings along the way, and we do our best to correct, or at least learn from them as well.

There are times when we are faced with difficult or challenging situations that we would rather turn around and run in the opposite direction; avoiding a confrontation seems to be the better course of action. We might feel that since we were all put on earth to help and love each other, a confrontation seems to be contrary to Unconditional Love we are supposed to feel for one another.

But we remember that every experience and challenge with which we are presented is a learning experience to be better appreciated not only along the way, but when we face our destiny as well. We might find that our life's work time requires a greater degree of responsibility that what we may be presently capable of handling; such a lesson might be one which involves a greater courage.

While there might be times when retreat out of spiritual strength is indeed the better course of action, there are others when the problem will not go away if it is ignored. In fact, it might only become worse. People might become more aggressive if they think that we are weak, especially if malice and intent is the primary motivation behind their aggression.

When faced with such situations, then, we need to rise and meet it head-on: We allow Spirit to act justly through us. Hence, our response is not borne out of aggression. Rather, ours is one of assertion, for we seek justice in the Universal sense. To do so requires a great deal of courage, for sometimes our human mind, motivated by ego, might want to act contrary to the laws of Universal justice. But to rise to the challenge of ego versus Spirit is one of the greatest acts of courage known to humankind.

- - - - -

There is Justice.
But Courage comes before Justice,
and Fairness should never be assumed.

As we remember, courage, or the ability to follow through with a plan of action, is demonstrated in the strength of the mind or body and will in the face of the challenging situation. Having returned to Square One with this definition, we now can appreciate its meaning from the Universal perspective.

From this aspect, we perceive fairness from the human aspect, justice from the Universal level.

Fairness is a concept unique to the eyes of each individual: What seems fair and right to one person may be totally the opposite to another. The answer to the question of fairness, then, depends upon who is asked in any given situation.

When we perceive justice from the Universal level, however, we find that such an application imposes no limitations or exceptions from the narrow-minded human perspective. Justice in Universal Law remains the same for everyone in the sense that all circumstances, intentions and actions are considered, and results are not meant as punishment, but as opportunities to balance any negative actions. What we would wish for ourselves we would wish for others, for the intent is based upon the Universal law of Unconditional Love and forgiveness.

As we already know, this does not mean that we must make ourselves a doormat for someone who seeks to walk over us and take advantage of us. But there is no punishment due us in sending back the negative that is wished upon us by our aggressors, but we must not do so with malice or intent to harm. We do it with a sense of honor and Universal justice, and realize that the consequences of any negative actions inflicted upon us will be determined by Universal law.

It is our duty and requirement, as Spiritual Warriors, to release the negativity inflicted upon us, however, difficult that might be, and forgive unconditionally.

- - - - -

On crossing the finish line
before we start:

Long before we came to the earth plane, we existed as one with the Universe. We lacked for nothing, for we lived in complete harmony, peace and love. We know, too, that we will return there as well, once we have accomplished everything needed to attain our destiny.

Knowing the perfection of our existence before we were born and that this perfection will again be ultimately attained, we sometimes might wish we were there now, especially when we are faced with adversity, difficult challenges, or when our responsibilities overwhelm us. Similarly, if we consciously know the nature of our destiny upon birth, we probably would not take the opportunity to savor the positive moments in the Now: We would be busy trying only to return to the state of Universal existence, possibly taking the easiest and quickest ways around any obstacles we might encounter. Not only could we miss learning our own personal lessons needed toward the attainment of our destiny, but we might create additional karma as well, especially if we run from any situations we might be required to face directly.

Most importantly, then, the one goal common to all of us is to love each other unconditionally and help each other when help is sought and requested. If we were in a hurry, we would not accomplish any of this, and we would miss the most important lesson of all.

- - - - -

Timid and wavering . . .
This is a continuum of our human nature.
Afraid of the shadow side,
handling the unexpected as if we will never move forward.
Seeing the Universal gifts of clear sight, clear hearing, and
Peace
like an unwelcome houseguest,
frightened because we just don't deserve anything.

This kind of thinking will keep us stuck at a dead end
with the road to the right and the left, but just standing, waiting,
confused by our own frailty, wondering when and if we should move
forward.
Lessons are learned when we come to the realizations
that we can no longer stand for our beliefs that were taught in infancy
of our life.

So now we must face the infancy of our souls, renewed, reborn,
ready not to repeat history.
Change, life and consistent movement toward the Energy, the Light,
the Completed knowingness.
No longer harboring all the undesired natter.[1]

Now, it is time to address our destiny, our birthright,
reaching for the senses that were never gone.
No theologian[2] can ever provide peace—it's just an openness.
I am not disputing the need for some whose beliefs differ. I am disput-
ing the fact
that all we are is not utilized to its fullest potential.
This is where the path is clear, and the balance between what's real
and what isn't, lies.

---

[1] To talk idly; chatter. American Heritage College Dictionary, 3rd Ed., Houghton Mifflin Co., 1997.

[2] One who has studied an organized system of faith and worship.

It speaks to us from the
skies:
One Voice.
Knowing, it beckons.

We are like children,
frightened of the dark.
Finding the Light is a welcome relief.
The pathway through the shadow side of our nature
into
the spiritual side of our Self.

Don't bring anything along.
You came in alone; you'll leave alone,
but the important thing
is what you have done along the way.
Tears cleanse your heart.
Fear cannot penetrate the inner soul, only the outer shell
and in the inner soul is where all these answers lie.

New Beginnings are like
the fresh rays of sunlight in the morning,
crisp and free.

We are beautiful, but the unwanted influence
of what we were in previous time beckons us
to change our self so that we can progress and
leave this place of unrest,
reaching for the far corners
of the Universal Spirit beyond where the Angels wait,
a place where none of us can fathom,
because we haven't excelled in our knowingness.

We have not used the tools we have.

Speak words in our minds:
one thought to another,
one soul to another.
A feeling.
Telepathy.
That kind of peace -
the kind that a smile brings.
It costs nothing to do these things,
but we'd rather sit and ponder than progress.

This is your challenge:
sense it, feel it.
Know it,
speak it:
Share it.

Five things that count.
This is the way
to begin opening all of yourself.

- - - - -

PART IV

WATER:
WHERE IT ALL BEGINS

Enlightenment in its Truest form
is Salvation

Mired by our own frailties,
feeling unworthy
of Universal freedom.
Open the path,
the Light is already on.

No time to distance one from another.
The energy must flow from within,
healing each heart with the compassion
of your grandmother's love.
Frightened to open all your resources
as if time stands still.

Move out of yourself
away from the ego into
the Warrior shielded with all the
Power that encompasses.
Embrace your destiny,
you have the quiet inner strength
to reach your full potential.

Three days before his return, she developed a sore throat.
Where did this come from? she wondered.

- - -

It was Friday night, and late. Though he had just flown back
into town, each had gone ahead and done their usual separate
activities. She hadn't wanted to pick him up at the airport
because she didn't want to see him just yet. She had been, and
was still angry: the night before, he called her on two separate
occasions to tell her how much he missed her, and in her eyes,
the words didn't quite ring true.

Though she felt he probably did miss her in his own way, he
had voluntarily spent two consecutive weeks with friends on two
different vacations, without her. So if he was going to tell her
again how much he missed her upon his return, she was going to
challenge him. If he missed her so much, how come he didn't
stick around? Not that it really mattered anymore. But was the
argument that would surely follow worth the effort of having it?

They were in bed now, and she was exhausted. She wanted
to go to sleep.

I missed you, he said softly, moving toward her.

Though she was angry, she hoped she would choose her
words carefully.

Yes, she said, you've been out for awhile! Pausing, she
added, but you had your choices and you made them.

He seemed puzzled, perhaps wondering what she meant.
His mind was on having an intimate evening.

But she was not going to let the matter drop. We work hard
for our money, she began. You waited five years to go on the
week-long trip, and it was great that you finally got to go! Then,
you were gone the next weekend, which was just before this
business trip. Granted, we're busy during the week, but the one
night you said we should do something together, you didn't
come home until 12:30 the next morning. And then you expect
me to be all happy to see you now?!

He was silent.

She was just getting warmed up. There was a time when I
should have said, 'Please spend some time with me,' she continued. But I didn't have enough sense of my self to say it. And
after awhile, I realized, what would we do together anyway? We

don't have anything in common, except skiing. And last year, after I had my surgeries, we couldn't even do that together. So you went ahead on your vacations. But that was okay, because that's what you wanted to do. I understand -

This is a fine Welcome Back! he muttered, obviously disgusted. Pausing, he added softly, But I understand your point. . .

There was nothing more to say.

The argument wasn't finished, but the mood was destroyed.

She was relieved. Why should she have to do something that had long ago lost its meaning for her?

Neither slept very well that night.

- - -

Shall we continue the discussion? he asked the next morning as he walked into their bedroom. It was 6:30 a.m. She was still in bed; he'd spent the night on the living room sofa, half-dozing, half-watching TV.

Why do you keep pushing me away! he began, lying down on the bed next to her. I gave you your freedom, let you have your space. I did everything I thought was right, and it still didn't work!

What didn't work? she wondered.

You know, I did enjoy going to the museum with you, he continued, remembering that she had a cultural streak in her. We need to do things together. Whatever you want to do would be great. . .

It was true that she hadn't invited him to her activities. Part of the reason was because she had needed her space. She was a much different person when he wasn't around, more outgoing, friendly, curious in a positive way. But the other reason she hadn't invited him was because she didn't think he'd be interested in her activities. He'd never shown any interest in those types of activities before.

She was beginning to get confused. She had started out so sure of herself, and now he was agreeing with her! There was nowhere left to go with this argument. Silence now filled the air.

Yes, she conceded, speaking slowly, wondering what was going to come out of her mouth next. You are right. When you were out on weeknights years ago and you did call, you would invite me to come, and I'd say no. And after awhile, you'd stopped asking. Who wouldn't, after hearing No so many times?

What she was saying was true, and both of them knew it. But she had chosen this battle because she had somehow felt justified in doing so. And now, despite the mutual agreement, something was still wrong; something had to come from this.

I love you so much, he said softly. I need you. I depend on you for my stability and well-being.

I can't do that for you. You can't rely upon anyone or anything to give that to you, she said automatically. She paused momentarily. This discussion was taking off in its own direction; a light was beginning to shine through the door that had almost closed.

What would you do if I died? she asked suddenly. In a sense, I'm already dead to him, she thought to herself.

I would deal with it, he responded in a monotone.

If he depended upon her solely for that stability that he should have found within himself, then this was his issue alone. There was nothing she could do about it.

You need to find stability and well-being within yourself. No one else can give that to you, she repeated softly.

The rest would be up to him.

In the aftermath of this argument, she felt shaken, unsettled. She hadn't wanted to bring up this uncomfortable issue and stayed around in the aftermath. She'd wanted to pack up and run away. But there was nowhere to run, and somehow she knew that whatever issue was left between them was not finished anyway. But what was there left to say now?

Silently, they retreated to their own separate worlds. There was a strained sense of discomfort in the air for the rest of the weekend.

- - -

It was once again Monday, and like all the other Mondays for the past couple of years, she was relieved to see it come. She realized that the issue would surface again, but already she was feeling better about it.

Though they continued to get along just fine together in their own separate worlds, daily they were moving further apart. In her world with him in it, she was unhappy; with her in his, he could act as though his was in order. But the telltale passion between them had somehow long ago faded and died; for her, it was painfully apparent. And for her, there was nothing that could bring it back.

She suddenly realized that they would continue for awhile longer, walking in opposite directions, he believing she was pushing him away, she wondering how and when it would all end. . .

But somewhere during that weekend, what was once her hope had been transformed into her faith: by the strength and the courage of her convictions, she was now confident within herself that her present situation would change.

- - -

Setting goals:
What do we want?

From the aspect of Spirit, our bodies might be relatively young, but our spirits, the essence of who we are, are very old. If we never seriously consider who we are or what we want to do in our lives, our souls begin to cry out to be heard.

The totality of our selves is connected through the mind, body and spirit. If the mind does not heed the soul's subtle promptings, the physical body ultimately becomes affected in some way. If we remain unbalanced for a long period of time, we may eventually shut down altogether. For our own survival, then, we need to set goals, or dreams of how we'd like our lives to be. These goals will allow us to rise up to the level of our destiny: Working toward them will assist in bringing us closer to our full potential and increasing a positive attitude within ourselves.

To begin formulating our goals, or the dreams of how we want our lives to be, we begin by listing everything we'd like to see or accomplish one year from now, professionally, emotionally and personally. Write them down, remembering to

1. Use the present tense;
2. Be positive;

3. Be specific; and
4. Formulate an action plan.

Using the present tense when stating our goals reminds us that everything happens in the Now, especially when considered from the aspect of Universal time.

Being positive means that we contemplate our desires without negativity, which includes loss of temper, or some other type of negative emotion. If we are in some way negative, we have lost our sense of self and self-respect as well as the loss of our self-control. We need to remember that any negative energy only manifests itself in negative behavior; similarly, emotions are a hair-trigger response to some underlying issue that needs to be explored more fully.

We must be specific about what we want: make it real! But if a particular goal seems overwhelming, we can remember that we don't have to do it right now, we simply think about what we want to do. Though we may not be ready to act, the energy embodied in our goal is released to Universe. Through time and circumstance, the right opportunities will present themselves to us, when and if we are ready, and if it was meant to happen.

Formulating an action plan allows us to consider what our exact course of action might be. Hence, we answer the question, What will it take to get there?

So when we are prepared, we contemplate a goal, and jot down one step daily toward its achievement, for seven consecutive days.

Defining Our Goals: the Process

Goals are sometimes not precisely defined overnight. Sometimes, defining our goals can become a goal in itself! Hence, we seriously contemplate the quality and nature of each one.

If we decide that one of our goals might be "I want to be happy," we might limit our progression, for such a goal tells us that we are not happy now. If we experience happiness at one point in our lives and feel that we are not happy now, then the kind of happiness we presently seek might not be sufficient to meet our needs. Hence, the goal becomes limiting in the long run: Such a goal might imply that happiness is, in itself, a transient state that comes and goes either by our moods, circumstances, or a combination of both.

How can we build toward something that limits us in the Now?

We need to remember that everything we have is in the Now. Again, it is all a matter of how we view the concept of Time.

A better goal, then, would be, "I want to be at peace with me."

- - - - -

Keeping a journal:
a chronology

Though we may not understand what's happening at the time, there's always the search...

- - - - -

One of the most important things we can do to define our goals is to keep a journal. Through consistent and daily practice, the journal becomes not only a chronology to document the events in our lives, but with the passage of time, we can also see the significance and impact of these events as our lives unfold. We can also appreciate the spiritual growth and the wisdom we have attained; when we examine our lives as illustrated by the words in our journal, we allow ourselves an opportunity for self-support, self-confidence, and attunement to our Higher Self.

To begin, we will name the journal "the book of gratitude," for the energy we put out to the world returns to us: we do this with a sense of harmlessness, in the Divine order of things and for the greatest good of all. Hence, we then invite positive and constructive events to manifest in our lives.

But from time to time, we do face difficult challenges, for there are lessons we need to learn from a Consciousness greater than our own: no one's life is without difficult challenges. Regardless, from the journal, we can see the growth and appreciate a greater strength to take the necessary steps toward a beneficial resolution. We can progress and move to a higher level.

To begin recording in your journal, think of an incident that happened during the day. Describe it, and its outcome. Consider the episode from these aspects: how you really felt about it; what insights you gained, or what you would have liked to have learned from it, and how you believed others saw you in this situation.

What made you grateful about that incident?

Even if the incident was particularly difficult or challenging, we can always find something positive within the negative, however insignificant the positive might seem. It might be that somebody else's behavior showed us how we don't want to act or be; sometimes the positive is found solely within ourselves. We can then feel grateful that the incident allowed an opportunity for observation or self-growth. If we feel as though we have not have acted in the manner ideal for a beneficial outcome, we can at least appreciate the fact that we are aware of how we would have liked to have acted, and that we have options and choices for our actions.

Keeping a journal doesn't need to be time-consuming or tedious. Sometimes, the entry might consist of one word or a feeling–whatever is significant in the moment. We are documenting where we are in the Now.

When we later review our entries, we can see that everything happens for a reason, in its own time, and that we are always meant to learn something along the way.

- - -

Facing the Truth About Ourselves And Not Retreating

What haven't we learned?

No doubt, some of our goals include issues surrounding the quality and nature of our relationships, for it is a basic human need to connect with one another. Our relationships, however, can be just as frustrating as they are rewarding. If we are having difficulties in our relationships, we can attain much of our spiritual growth by working through the issues and understand what we must do to resolve them.

Our attempts to connect with each other begin with our attitude toward ourselves: When we have our self-respect, self-confidence, and a sense of responsibility for ourselves and others in order, we can attract people who nurture success in our lives.

Below are six common behaviors that inhibit our self-growth and in some manner, affect our relationships. Most likely, not all of these will apply. However, some of them, and perhaps others which are not listed here, might be relevant:

Do we (perhaps subconsciously) encourage others to feel sorry for us?

Do others continually motivate and encourage us, attempting to build us up?

Do others give us attention and compliments as if they are trying to make us feel good about ourselves and our actions?

Do we avoid doing things because others might dislike us, or perceive us as a threat or competition to them?

Do we avoid doing things so we do not have to risk failure?

Are our unpleasant behaviors or habits justified because others know we lack self-esteem?

The above list, and any other possibilities as well, can be considered payoffs, for if we demonstrate this behavior, some type of benefit, even at the expense of someone else, is attained. But these payoffs ultimately take our power from us, instead of strengthening it, for they will not fill the heart or nourish the spirit. They will throw us off-balance, and where there is no balance, there is no peace. But we can change these behaviors, and in doing so, we will bring the mind-body-spirit connection into sync. Ultimately, we will find our inner peace and reclaim our power.

What helps us forward?

As painful as it might be, we need to be honest about our emotions, for they generate most of our actions. We need to ask ourselves: Are we manipulating the others in our lives to achieve a payoff of sorts, or are we allowing their behavior to manipulate us? We can gauge ourselves by our reactions resulting from their actions.   We can also examine the intent behind our actions, as well as the result. Are we building confidence, or ego? Are we seeking empathy in the form of a handup, or sympathy in the form of a handout? Do we make errors or mistakes?

- - - - -

Are we building confidence, or ego?

Confidence is built through experience; it is shaken as we grow and dream; our fears, as powerful as they might seem, must be minimized. We need to stop pretending that we are more confident than we actually are, and we must be honest about the ways we avoid facing our insecurities. When we are confident, we are not frightened of failure; we are powerful beyond measure.

Similarly, we must not ignore, nor must we allow ourselves to minimize our dreams, for when we discount them, or dream small, we are only shortchanging ourselves. We can grow only as much as our dreams will allow.

We must not allow fear to rule our lives. Our fear is simply an illusion; we must not allow it to become a reality. We must make the Light a beginning point to dispel the fear. First, we resolve the conflict within us; usually, anger or some other powerful emotion indicates that there is a conflict. Once we are aware of the conflict, however, we must address it. We can interpret (irrational) fear as a sign to move forward, not as one to stop doing what we're doing. We must not shut down, nor should we allow fear to incapacitate us.

If we are having ego-related issues, we should question whether we need to demonstrate to the rest of the world that we are in some way superior. If we do not believe in ourselves, but show the rest of the world that we are believable, we somehow come up empty, constantly seeking the approval from others that we cannot obtain from within ourselves.

Learning to rise above the ego involves the decision to progress spiritually. Such a decision requires commitment and responsibility to our total self (the essence of who we are in mind-body-spirit) and to others for the good of all involved. We need to be positive, maintain a listening and empathic awareness, and an openness to commitment. We must have faith, trust, and an ability to listen to ourselves, for all the answers we will ever need can come from Within.

- - - - -

Are we seeking empathy in the form of a handup, or sympathy in the form of a handout?

A handout is given with no strings attached: Hence, we are not required give anything in return for what we have received. In contrast, we seek a handup in an attempt to rise to a greater level.

Similarly, do we give a handout to others because we feel sorry for them, thereby placing ourselves on a superior level? Or do we give a handup with the intent of helping them, and allowing them to take a responsibility to utilize the gift and seeking self-determination and independence in return?

While we can give a handout without any strings attached, again, it is the intent behind the gift that matters: We give from the heart, in the spirit of compassion for the other. And if someone gives us an unsolicited handout, we can accept it, knowing that we can someday pass the kindness along to someone else.

- - -

We can determine whether our misdeeds are errors or mistakes when we consider our intent, and the circumstances behind the action which resulted in an unfavorable outcome. Mistakes are made when we haven't changed our behavior; they can be repetitive in nature. An error, however, is a wrong ultimately committed even when we had a positive intent and used our best impressions to accomplish the task. Though both can be corrected, mistakes can prove more costly in the long run.

- - - - -

Moving forward -

We bring positive results into our world when we are true to ourselves, from the aspect of harmlessness, not only toward others, but to ourselves as well. There are certain beliefs we must hold within ourselves, that will allow for positive and beneficial changes: We must believe in our ability to find love, understanding and compassion in all situations, especially the difficult ones. We must believe in our ability to connect with other human beings in a loving and meaningful way, and we must believe in our ability to know that what we have to offer others as a spiritual human being is valuable.

And when the time is right, we attract others into our lives that can enhance the self we were truly meant to be: We will encounter our soul mates or soul partners.

- - - - -

Soul Mates and Soul Partners:
We are not alone.

When we are presented with Life's greatest challenges, we may find help from those whom we ultimately recognize as our soul mates or our soul partners. Though we may have contact with many others during the course of our lives, the soul mates or partners are the ones who have the greatest significance and most profound effect upon us.

Our soul mate or mates are meant to assist us with our life's lessons; they appear in our lives when needed. We may meet one, or several soul mates; they could be our closest associates, best friends, parents, children or other relatives, or perhaps they are our lovers or spouses. They may remain with us throughout our lives, or they may leave us when their tasks, or ours, or both, are finished. Perhaps they may reappear from time to time, depending upon the situation, timing and circumstances. Our relationship with the soul mate may be harmonious or it may be tumultuous; if it is the latter, it may be that our tasks involve ongoing issues that need resolutions.

When one soul, on a spiritual level, recognizes another, the soul partner is recognized. We have one only; it is as if two separate physical entities have split apart from a single soul: The love between the two is unconditional. Regardless of the circumstances in which two partners might find themselves at any given time, it is the partner that is the other half of the soul: we are continually drawn back to them.

As with soul mates, however, soul partners may have issues that need resolutions, for our actions do not always express who we are now, or who we are meant to be at a later time.

The connection between soul partners is almost always on the physical level (either hetero- or homosexual). However, when the souls are highly advanced, the connection could be on a spiritual level only, or even one from beyond the veil.

If we have not yet found our soul mate or partner (or perhaps we have, but have not yet recognized them as such), we might find ourselves wondering whether we will ever find them. Out of frustration, we may have resigned ourselves to the fact that we will always be alone.

But the Universe is not that cruel.

Even though we were born alone and we will die alone, and each of us must individually pursue our chosen destiny, we were not meant to be alone forever, for it is most likely that we will encounter at least one soul mate in our lifetime, if not our soul partner.

The plan of Life is ordered through the Universe, and so for any such encounters, we must be ready, for as we already know, the events in our lives occur as a result of Universal time and circumstances. Sometimes, we are required to progress or attain certain goals before we meet a soul mate or partner. Sometimes, they are not yet ready to meet us.

It is possible, too, that we have already met our soul partner, but we were separated and found ourselves with a soul mate when the partner suddenly reappears in our life. Or perhaps we are with a soul mate when we are introduced to our partner, leaving us to wonder how and why we came to be where we are in the Now. Regardless of our situation, if we find ourselves alone and wish to bring a soul mate or partner into our lives, we must decide that we are not alone forever. We must affirm in our hearts and minds that we are ready to step out in faith and belief;

we must demonstrate to the Universe that, when time and circumstances are right, that we are ready for that meeting.

Most importantly, we must trust our intuition: If we have not yet met our mate or partner, we must realize that when we do, we will know in our hearts. Through our own clarity and instincts, we will be confident that one soul, if not both, will always recognize the other first.

- - - - -

Quality Relationships

Our relationships with our soul mates, partners or significant others are meant to be positive, constructive and enhancing, both for ourselves, and for the other. However, we may feel that our relationships somehow fall short of what we think they should be. If this is so, we need to determine the issues. We need to ask ourselves:

Is one person dominant over another?

An even energy exchange promotes the most beneficial kind of relationship. If this is not the case, we somehow give away our dignity. We lose pieces of ourselves, and in a sense, we reduce ourselves to whatever happens. Most often, the result is shame, which, along with anger, fear and guilt, has no place in our lives. If we come to realize that we have been dominated and are no longer willing to accept the situation, we need to have the strength to move out it and the emotional ties which have limited our positive growth. Do we have the strength to create a place within ourselves where there is no shame?

Are we reacting or interacting with the other?

If we tend to react instead of interact, we need to ask ourselves, What are we reacting from? Emotions create reactions; they are triggers to some deeper issue. If we find that either we, or our significant other is in some way reacting, we need to determine the reasons behind it. In a non-threatening way, we need to address the issues with the other, and when doing so, we must remain flexible to re-evaluate whatever needs to be addressed.

Have we been hurt by this person before?

If the answer to this question is Yes, we need to understand why we remain with them by listening to the answers coming from our inner self. Are we receiving any warnings or negative feedback about them in the Now? Are they draining us of our energy? Are we doing something positive, meaningful and con-structive, both for ourselves and with them? Or do we serve as an ornament or a status symbol for them, or they for us? Becoming someone we are not is not compromising; we will only lose pieces of ourselves if we do so.

Do we experience more pain than pleasure from this person?

The answer to this question requires honesty, respect, and commitment. If we realize that the answer is Yes, we end up feel-ing used, abused and foolish.

Whether we are aware of this for a long time, or if we sud-denly become aware, we must take our responsibility in the situ-ation if we allow it to go on. We were not meant to live our lives in pain; the next question we must ask is Why are we still in the relationship?

As we are already well aware, there are reasons we stay where we are; but always we need to be aware of them and the issues we face by staying in the situation. Whatever the reasons, whether they be about timing or a combination of extenuating circumstances, we must accept what we cannot change and be aware that when the time, or circumstances are right, we will do what we must to for the betterment of ourselves, and for the greatest good of all.

- - - - -

Bring forth the courage
to take a stand.
The balance comes in
when you think you can.

Weary from
lessons
given and taught
life is complex.
Don't be fearful:
help from the Universe
is a song of joy -

Relationships are not measured in time, but by our lessons learned.

If we have realized that our relationship is no longer working in a way that is positive and constructive for us, we may decide to change our situation by moving out of it. Or perhaps that decision has already been made for us by the other, with their expressed desire to leave.

Regardless of any given situation, the path through it, for the greatest good of all, can be painful and lengthy process. But it can also be a time of growth and self-discovery. Though we may not be able to change the situation, or change it in the time we desire, we can change ourselves during the time we must wait. If we remember to seek the positive within the negative, it will be less difficult to find our way through it, for things do have a way of working out. And when done with grace and in the Divine right time, we will do it right, and for the greatest good of all.

Going with the flow:
Life closes doors in rooms where we are,
and we get stuck in the moment...

...Seek the Lesson in the Moment.

When we realize that a door is closing and we are ready for a change, we may find that we are unable to move forward; the door to our future is locked. Despite our goals, despite the positive energy we have put out there, despite our plans for a better future, we remain stuck where we are. If we believe that it's over and there's nothing left, then why are we still there?

First, we need to figure out our own issues about the situation, and, once they have been determined, we need to ask: What is the lesson for us?

Sometimes, the issues are recurring; the lesson involves repetition of the circumstances. But after we have resolved them the first time, the solution next time around becomes easier. To an extent, we can control them by our own behavior. We can also measure our growth by asking ourselves: How well did we learn the lesson? Perhaps the lesson is on a much deeper level than we had initially realized.

We also need to remember that we are only one small facet of the bigger picture: The lessons are not always about us. Perhaps it is the issue of the other one involved. He or she might not be ready to move forward; perhaps they might come out of it better or stronger for the patience or skill we are required to demonstrate. Sometimes we are there simply to give them needed strength and support as they wait for the next chapter of their lives to begin. Our role, then, could be one of teacher, or the student to learn some lesson we are required to discover, but most often, we are both teacher and student, for there is always something to learn. And sometimes there isn't any hidden agenda: Perhaps the time to move on has not yet come.

But as we deal with any situation, we must remember to ride with the pain and keep our balance as we do so. We must not take other people and other things for granted; they might be a part of the lesson as well.

Regardless of the lesson, we need to remember that sometimes bad things do happen to good people: The Universe sometimes hands us life-changing events to put us on a different path. But it's the way we deal with them that counts, and to realize that through the situation we encounter our lessons, even though the knowledge contained within the lesson itself may not come until later, after we have transcended the suffering and endured the situation through to its final conclusion.

But if we do find ourselves stuck in any difficult situation or relationship, we must remember that patience is required: We must not become self-centered or strive for instant gratification or an easy way out for ourselves. Life brings us to our knees with a purpose in mind; the lesson we learn takes us to a different level of our spiritual growth. Most importantly, we must keep our sanity while the lesson unfolds; we need to transcend the ego and rise above the anger and fear. But always, the lesson is about more than just dumping the garbage: It is about finding the balance.

Doing what's right, fixing what's wrong

By nature, we are nurturers, unless we were somehow damaged in our youth. We try to heal the wounds inflicted upon us when we were very young by attracting people into our lives that reflect our own needs because what we put out there does return to us.

From childhood into adulthood, many of us had shut down along the way to deal with the pain; somehow the pain remained locked inside, unable to get out. If left there too long, we may not now be able to express our thoughts or feelings without imploding or exploding. If this is an issue, we need to understand the pain by asking ourselves, Where do our thoughts or feelings begin? Where do they end? As we have already learned, the answers begin come as we discover the intent behind our actions and how they affect our relationships. They also come through the others around us. We watch them, or listen to what others tell us along the way.

When we are consciously aware of our attempts to evolve, then there's hope. Knowledge is power; realizing this is a key to the first step in the process. Acceptance of where we are is tantamount to the journey. To do so, we need to separate ourselves from our ego and our emotions, especially the anger. If it's stuffed inside, there's no room left to grow. We must emotionally distance ourselves to make good choices, for the greatest benefit of all. In releasing the negativity, we allow ourselves the wisdom and opportunity for right action: We reclaim our power that is our birthright.

- - - - -

Effective Conflict Resolution: There is Peace When We Get Past the Pain.

If there is a conflict within our relationship that needs to be constructively addressed, we do so by sticking to the facts, and address the issues in a non-threatening manner. But we also need to pick and choose our battles, the timing, and the reasons for the battle. And if the issue involves the behavior of the other person, we allow a constructive assessment without a character assassination.

As expected, we need to consider our intent and the reasons for our dissatisfaction. Are we addressing the issues because we have an agenda, or are we attempting to initiate a plan? If we have an agenda, we may be leaning more toward exclusive self-gain; if ours is a plan, we might instead anticipate a step toward a more balanced relationship or at least a workable resolution for all parties involved.

If the issues are emotionally charged (as they usually are), we will need to choose our words carefully and keep as calm as possible, for by our actions and words, we demonstrate who we are. In the heat of an argument, we cannot help but experience our emotions, especially anger, but we can at least step back and think before we speak or act. While anger is generally perceived as a negative emotion, it can have its positive aspects when we view it as a gauge to what we are feeling inside. It can also serve as an impetus to action, when combined with right timing and purpose.

Even if the issues are those which bring us to a crossroads in the relationship, the Universe does reward right action and behavior. Sometimes there is nothing we can do to mend a fractured relationship, except to bring the issues to light and further the path toward its final conclusion. Nevertheless, we must discuss the issues with honesty and integrity.

Always, we remember to Do unto others as we would have them do unto us.

- - - - -

If it is the other who initiates the grievance, we can remember that things do happen for a reason, and the time to address the issues was right for them, even if the time may seem inappropriate to us. The first thing we must do is listen as they share the issue or their pain with us. A listening attitude implies that the spiritual side of us seeks the resolution: Without the ego or emotions, our first thought comes from Spirit. We remain open to allow Spirit to come through, for if the spiritual self is not reacting, the emotional self will. We then address their concerns with attention, acceptance and appreciation.

We pay attention to what the other says with awareness on all levels, acceptance that allows us to realize that if we cannot fix it, to let it go, and appreciation that we understand the lesson presented within the situation. Always, it is the journey, not the destination, that matters, for it is the journey that allows the spiritual side of us to grow.

- - - - -

If we find ourselves at a stalemate, a good way to get beyond it is to accept, accommodate and acknowledge the issues. At this point, we have already acknowledged that an issue needs to be addressed; we accept the fact that we can either fix the problem or let it go. If we can accommodate the requests of the other, then, we will find that a compromise is an effective resolution. A compromise implies that something is given up, concessions are made by both or all parties, and a workable solution is achieved.

When we consider the meaning of the word compromise as a mutual promise, we also realize that a promise indicates a debt unpaid. If a compromise is balanced, it should be a fair exchange for both. When stating our desires for a resolution, then, we need to be clear about what we want. Both parties should walk away from the disagreement feeling satisfied with the concessions they must make.

Since we need our own self-respect as well as respect for the other, we must make certain that the compromises we make are those which we can truly honor. We must not sacrifice our honesty and integrity, nor must we allow it to take pieces of ourselves that we are unwilling or unable to relinquish. If the result of the compromise is anger, then the compromise is not acceptable. The question becomes, then, How much of ourselves are we willing to relinquish? If we give too much and feel that we receive little in exchange, would the balance in their favor rob them of some responsibility they need to assume?

- - - - -

If we are not accustomed to speaking out and addressing the issues, especially calmly and without emotion, stating our side of the issues can be difficult. Many of us were brought up to be nice, often at the cost of our self-esteem. If this true, we might be stepping out of the ego, the learned process to accommodate being nice, if we stand up and be heard. We need to step back, plan what we are going to say, gather the courage to rise to the occasion, and then do it. Though we can expect to feel uncomfortable, we don't need to put ourselves down. Rising to the Higher self is a learned process–it doesn't happen overnight! We must not criticize or judge ourselves too harshly; we don't have to solve everything at one time. We must also remember that men and women think and communicate differently: Women tend to be more verbal. We were all raised with different expectations, and each of us has various styles when addressing and resolving the issues.

If, when expressing ourselves, the other individual won't allow us the opportunity to speak, we can try the phrase, "I need you to listen to me." Allow them time to digest this statement. You should be allowed their silence while you express your concerns; you have at least given them that opportunity to grow and evolve.

But if they are neither ready or willing to listen, or constructively discuss the issues, and instead blame us or take offense to the issues, search for hidden motives or meanings, or jump to irrational conclusions, we have to work through it to get beyond

it. We must be able to see the negative behavior; it is not our role
to be manipulated or buy into any emotional blackmail. The
negative energy doesn't belong to us, and we must not allow it
to gather strength and take us down.

Even in the heat of the argument, what would it resolve if we
expend our energy? Is it a gift we would want to give them?
Similarly, their negative energy doesn't belong to us. We need to
distance ourselves emotionally, and draw our own boundaries.
Otherwise, some piece of our foundation is gone. As difficult as it
might be at the time, we need to stand tall. Do we have the
courage of our convictions?

During, and after we have finished the conversation, we need
to relax and take deep breaths to alleviate any fear and anxiety.
We react out of fear and loss of control; breathing deeply will
continue the flow of concentration and confidence.

Sometimes the situation has no resolution, and if that is the
case, we must at least seek a conclusion: We must never leave a
disagreement without our dignity, and we must rise above the
anger, be it either ours or theirs. If the other is unwilling to
accept what has been demonstrated as an even exchange, it
becomes their lesson, and it becomes the gift of discernment
for both.

- - - - -

And if we truly cannot restore harmony with the other person, then we must restore our own balance. We cannot change
them, but we can change ourselves. After we have let the facts be
known, we need to let it go. Sometimes, all we can do is to at
least understand what the other is trying to express. The rest
becomes their issue.

- - - - -

Renewing the Spirit
is always painstaking
because of all the baggage
we bring with us from
one lifetime to the next.
We stand at a closed door
seeing, realizing it's not locked,
but terrified
to turn the knob
and step through.
We hurt ourself
by not allowing Spirit
to direct our path
and free us
from the endless journey
that only circles round, round.
Instead of looking straight ahead,
we perceive ourselves as
intelligent.
We grip the endless stream of
hope,
awaiting the unknown,
saying
The future will take care of
itself,
but still not doing anything
to assure our own peace of mind...

It's not Magic

So many people believe that their lives are always going to be caught in the crossroads of emotional turmoil, never to find any semblance of inner peace. Yet real life would show us that things always have a way of calming, as we end one series of events and begin anew.

But how do we find our way when all seems hopeless and we feel as though we are in the slow descent to hell?

I've always believed that things will change with the powers unseen all around us. For instance, consider a love lost and then dropping back into our life out of nowhere. What could possibly bring us to a place where we aren't in a continuum of old history, mixed with current emotion?

I believe that sometimes we should embrace this challenge without bringing up old hurts. Universally, we all connect in one way or another with the God light and the whole nucleus of power unseen by most, yet untouched by all, because we incapacitate ourselves with fear of moving forward. In a sense, we settle into our forgotten realm of yesteryear.

What if for once we just cleared the air, realizing we need a new beginning in order to grow and evolve?

Perhaps our progression is best supported when we remember the following:

We are human. To err is human; forgive is Divine: Forgiveness is a gift we give ourselves. We recognize that forgiveness means we no longer allow the old hurts to take away from us the power that is rightfully ours.

We don't always want to admit uncertainty, yet often this the best way to provide a safe place within ourselves to grow stronger.

We allow our ego to cost our values. How many times have we pretended to be something that we are not? We must be true to who we are.

We need one another for survival: No person is an island. We are all in some way connected to each other. This is why our very spiritual growth depends upon the quality of our relationships with others.

We cannot grow if stagnated by old, useless habits, karma,

and idle ego. But we can grow, when we transcend the self-limi-
tations of these habits, accept our responsibility for the karmic
issues and transcend the stagnated ego enough to allow the inner
peace to shine through.

We must move ever forward or die. Death of our spiritual
self is the worst and most crucial thing in which we will never
evolve to a place where true peace exists.

No wonder our pain begins at birth: We were born into it.
We have no other normal emotions!

Your guides don't ever want you to suffer from your own
demise. Reality is so clear if you only ask all of them for help.
They are out here just waiting for you to ask. Step out in faith,
without skepticism; free yourself! Your spiritual self is at stake.
Remember, there is more than what we see on this earth plane!
You may be frightened only if you fail to pay attention, if you
believe that they can't, or won't respond when you think they
should. Do not allow the human side of you to be fooled into not
wanting their help.

And when you seek their help, listen for the answer. Go with
Peace, with faith: know that the negativity will soon be gone.

- - - - -

Working through yesteryear
knowing my solace has come.
Remembering heartaches past
all behind me, done.

Smiling now because I'm free
no longer unsure of me
my Inner Voice has spoken

My Higher Self expanding
believing, knowing, trusting.

Life at home had its idyllic moments. At these times, nothing seemed to be wrong, and she wondered what had ever led her to believe that there was a problem in the first place? These were the moments she'd always cherish and remember long after the ashes were too cold to be stirred and the fire rekindled: before work, over cups of coffee, they would share and then discuss their dreams during the night, their meanings, and their significance. It was a harmonious feeling, a learning time, and to her it felt as though the busy world around paused for a just moment to smile.

Yet just below the surface of these tranquil times, something didn't seem quite right. She felt it, and sensed that he did, too. It seemed as though each wanted to be elsewhere, yet where, neither could precisely say. But they could see it in their dreams, feel it in the very air in the house where they were doing their best to peacefully coexist. Both were impatient to find out what that something was, but it also seemed that only time could provide the answers. For the present, then, she felt that they were caught between the very pages of this uncertain element, this Time factor.

But these tranquil stretches also allowed her the opportunity to wonder what was wrong with her instincts. He could be, and was, understanding and compassionate, exhibiting all the characteristics of the man she'd married so long ago. Perhaps I cannot see very clearly? she wondered. Perhaps we are so moody because the planets are radically shifting in the sky. Perhaps he isn't changing at all. Perhaps it is I who cannot get along. Perhaps. . .

But in the morning, she'd wander out to the kitchen and count the number of empty beer bottles he'd neatly lined up by the door from the night before, waiting for someone to put them into the recycling container.

- - -

And there were the times when they did argue. Not just the usual spats that people sometimes have because of a lack of communication or something involving the actions of the other person; these were not the "I-did-you-did" ones. These were major ones, the "who we are ones," ones that, for them, had no resolution. She didn't mind them, though, for at least she had proof that there indeed was something amiss, that everything wasn't as harmonious as it had appeared to be. These arguments simply confirmed what her intuition was telling her, and for that at least, she was gratified. She would deal with it as best she could until she figured out what to do.

She could learn something positive from these experiences, she felt. Her lessons, whatever it was she needed to do, could be determined by what was going on in the present. This could be a growing time for her, and for him, too. She would learn to accept, to understand, to become wiser with this Time at a seeming standstill.

- - -

And there were the times when she was angry, so angry to find herself where she was! She felt as though she'd awakened one morning and found that her world had changed overnight, leaving her with some strange man she only thought she knew, a man who was at war with himself, at her, angry at his own world, figuratively striking out at the shadows he had created around him, or whatever other target happened to be in his way. She felt as though she had been caught in the crossfire of a war in which there were no definable sides. Why was she even here? Why did she stay? What were her answers? Without them, she didn't know what to do.

Until that time, where could she go to seek refuge?

Where could she hide?

- - -

He had driven four hours nonstop to get back into town from his business trip, so he was beat. Why he had done that, she didn't know; his arrival had been a surprise to her. Since he hadn't called to let her know his itinerary and didn't normally do so anyway, she saw no need to drop everything she was doing just to welcome him home. Besides, she had things to do, and she was going to finish them that evening.

Silently, she worked at the kitchen sink, while he silently sat at the nearby table with a blank look on his face, or maybe he was just lost in thought. He appeared exhausted and frustrated. Not only had it been a long trip, but this particular job had been a rough one too, and there were a lot of unexpected and unwelcome developments that had accompanied it.

From his vantage point, sometimes he watched her, sometimes he stared into space. He had a troubled look on his face, but she suspected that if she asked him anything, he wouldn't say much of anything. The wordless energy expanded between them, stretching endlessly into the vast ocean that had come between them, separating each into a little island. It seemed now as though each was placed at opposite ends of the world they had once shared.

A long time ago, she would have welcomed this attention, his sitting here at the table. She would have asked all kinds of questions about the particular job he was doing, his trip, the people with whom he had worked, about everything that had happened. But that was a long time ago, he probably would not have sat in the kitchen back then. Instead, he would have caught up on his mail, called his friends, planned his weekend, and looking a lot happier.

But that was a long time ago, and things had indeed changed.

If it had even been a few weeks ago and he had sat in the kitchen while she worked there, she probably would have felt that he was intruding in her space, and she would have resented it. She would have wanted as much time alone as possible, wanting to hide instead of feeling as though she were being watched by this man who was fast becoming a stranger to her, an intruder into her own little private world she was fast building around herself.

Now, however, she felt that she was willing to accept whatever happened.

She grateful for the silence in the moment, for she could think of nothing to say. And as for his presence, she didn't think anything about it. Acceptance, she thought to herself. No more hiding, no more anger on my part. Simply be where we are because, for whatever reasons, we need to be there. Just be in the moment.

The minutes passed.

Call John and Gayna, she suddenly heard herself saying.

The sound of her own voice startled her, for she hadn't been consciously thinking about anything in particular, let along saying something. In her ears, her voice sounded a little too tinny, overeager, too abrasive to be helpful, and its very tone shattered that silent void that had finally overtaken the kitchen.

But she had suggested the call because he just seemed so sad, too quiet.

Maybe if he did something, she thought, if he felt the happy energy of friends, he'd feel better.

Perhaps he's beginning to notice that things seem a little strained between us. Perhaps we're too quiet. Perhaps he's beginning to see how different we are?

But maybe he's not noticing anything at all.

Whatever it was, he was just not moving away from the table. . .

Finally, he retreated to the bedroom to watch a little television.

The next morning, he had gotten out of bed slowly. One more day at work; why bother to be enthusiastic? It was evident that his mood hadn't changed.

What is with him? she wondered.

Like the visibility of an iceberg, only twenty percent of our thoughts come from the conscious mind. . .

What is with me? she suddenly thought. Why do I need to distract him? Am I doing this because I'm still hiding from him, or am I trying to be helpful?

Now she wondered what she was really thinking!

Silently she watched him, wanting answers to the questions that had not yet been asked.

- - -

It was one of those days where, had she not been through what she'd already endured, she would've gone mad.

She was at work that day, overwhelmed with the magnitude of work she had yet to finish, yet feeling powerful, strong enough to conquer whatever challenge might arise: She was also having one of those rare days when everyone and everything was in sync. Her clients, even her most difficult ones, agreed with whatever suggestions she made; she was accomplishing a lot. The partially-completed projects were finished and promptly mailed; the new ones, the seedlings, as she called them, began to grow rapidly, nurtured by her creative thinking. It was a rare, wonderful day...

And then he called.

Out of the blue, that voice, the one that had driven the knife into her heart and then slowly twisted it, the man who never came back because he was too scared of the commitment that each had just begun to recognize.

She sat there with the telephone in her hand, motionless, speechless, pieces of the day falling away as if somebody had begun to chisel away at it, the shards beginning to crack the ice that had long ago frozen around her heart.

But through the cold chill that had suddenly settled over her office, she began to feel the warm sun breaking through the rays. She started breathing again. Perhaps this was a sign of a new beginning, a better tomorrow? What had they learned through the passages of Time?

They agreed to meet at a restaurant after work on Friday.

- - -

She sat in the foyer, telling the host that she was waiting for somebody, feeling slinky in a beautiful, trendy flowered dress she'd bought especially for this occasion, this reunion. This was an expensive place; she was pleased that he'd suggested it. It said something about her, about them, she thought. They'd been good together before; it could happen again. But it was up to him.

She was nervous; time was passing slowly. She looked good, felt great. Apparently, the host saw that, too, for he smiled approvingly at her as she did her best to act as nonchalant as possible. It was rush hour, and there were several other people waiting in this area, too. Traffic was especially bad this evening.

Despite the years that had passed, she hadn't changed much on the outside, but inside, a transformation had taken place: She had been forced to take a good look within herself.

I'll be right back, he'd told her. But he never returned. Waiting for his return, she finally realized that he wasn't coming back. Her spirit was broken, the pieces scattered on the ground...
Why?

She sat, pondering the mystery as the others, one by one, happily disappeared with their loved ones. Would she be next? she wondered.

- - -

Forty-five minutes of waiting was long enough. Half-disappointed, partly-embarrassed, mostly angry, she stood up, smoothed out her dress, and walked toward the door. That old familiar heartache was beginning to overwhelm her; all over again she felt betrayed. The ice that had begun to crack around her heart was now beginning to tear into it, but she resolved to maintain her dignity until she reached the safety of her car.

Stepping outside, she was amazed that it was still so bright and sunny outside; she felt as though the sun was deluding her into believing that everything was going to be all right. Slowly, she made her way to the parking lot, which was fast filling up with the dinner crowd.

But when she reached her car, she had a feeling that something was left unfinished. Turning slowly around, she saw him, standing motionless behind her, as though Time had frozen him in place. The chemistry between them was the same, and it was obvious that he recognized it, too.

How've you been! he exclaimed, as though he'd seen her just this morning and he was just now coming back to take her to dinner. She felt as though she'd been caught in a time warp: he was acting as though he'd never left at all!

Had Time passed? she wondered.

She shook herself from her reverie long enough to hear him talking about his work, his life. Just a casual acknowledgment of the three years that had passed–My, how time flies! Didn't he remember that he had left her place, promising to return within a couple of hours and then suddenly dropping out of her life without as much as a goodbye or an explanation. It was as though he'd never even existed!

She nodded absently, acknowledging that she was listening to him, all the while not believing what she was either seeing or hearing.

But she was beginning to see the pattern repeating itself: she advancing, hoping; he retreating, throwing out the smokescreen and anything else he could think of, to cloud his true feelings. It was like some bizarre ritual.

False Rituals, she suddenly realized.

He is here because he is curious to see how I've changed, if I've changed. He is here because his business is failing, his life is falling apart. He needs a distraction. He had left me out of fear, discounting our love, running away from that something that had frightened him within his own heart.

They were two separate people, married in the spirit, but staring at the painting of Life through two different sets of eyes. What did he see? What did she believe? Could he even begin to comprehend how much she had loved him, how much she would have given her very life for his, how their love could have transcended any obstacles they would ever have encountered together? She stared deeply into those vacant, indigo eyes, wondering who was really in there. What did he really see?

Suddenly she realized that through the passage of Time, she was still struggling to make him love her. But how could she make him love her when he was incapable of loving even himself?

And then she heard him say, Know that this fool loved you even before he ever knew you...

Would he ever comprehend the meaning of those words?

For him, the same passages echoed with meaningless conversation, alive with the ghosts and shadows of his life. It was apparent that he'd learned nothing through his passage of Time, for although he'd suffered a few nasty blows in his business and personal life, the only thing he had allowed Time to bestow upon him were a few extra pounds on what had never been a lanky frame.

Yet in his own way he did love her, though his love would not, could not, reach the depths of hers for him. In some way he had grown, yet he held himself back, perhaps frightened of what he might find inside himself?

She knew that she would never again allow him to hurt her as he had before. Though she knew that they were married in spirit, for her own sake, his role in her life would be minimal, if she allowed him to be there at all.

If he only knew what he'd missed, she thought as she was leaving the parking lot of the restaurant. She clung to her dignity and her tears, until she was alone in the safety of her car. But when she finally allowed them to come, they began to mend the pieces of her tattered heart.

- - -

Moving beyond loss:
Our Heart is Strongest
where it was broken.

If our relationship has failed in some way and the time has come to move on, be it either by our own hand or theirs, we can take comfort in the fact that the pain will not last forever, and that there are various stages to the healing process, through which we pass. Our task at this time is to step out in faith and experience this process; we will get through it.

Following are nine phases through which we pass to heal the soul:

1. Denial: This cannot be happening.

To move beyond the denial, we must be aware of what is going on around us. We must acknowledge reality, as well as our feelings about what is happening. We must not dwell on the shame or embarrassment of what we have experienced or where we are in the Now.

2. Bargaining: Driving ourselves crazy.

We need to accept who we are, and who they are. If we cannot conform to the other's standards, we need to accept that as well. We cannot expect that our actions will produce the outcome we desire.

3. Loneliness: Feeling no one cares, or understands.

Relationships sometimes do break up, as much as we might desire otherwise. But we are not alone: we can surround ourselves with people who are supportive and positive. Positive energy does breed the positive; the pain won't last forever, even if it seems that way now!

4. Heartbreak: Feeling as if our heart is really breaking.

If the heart feels as though it is physically breaking, as sometimes is the case, we can lessen the pain if we rub a hand over the heart area to soothe it; the power of touch is a positive, healing experience. We might also take comfort in the fact that it is our experience that counts and it is our own efforts that will make us happy, even if others might discount what we are feeling.

5. Blame: Pointing the finger at ourselves or the other.
We must not blame ourselves, nor the other, for what has happened. It's all a learning experience, and from it, we grow.

6. Depression: Feeling worthless and foolish.
We need to allow ourselves to feel the pain, but we must not allow ourselves to wallow in self-pity. Just as positive energy breeds the positive, misery loves company.

7. Anger: Feeling furious.
Similarly, we must also allow ourselves to feel the anger, but we must not exaggerate it. We needn't relive the past, even if what we feel happened to us wasn't our fault. Our job is about stopping the fear within us, rising above it and expressing Self in a positive manner. We must not allow the other, or the situation the power to incapacitate us in our own anger.

8.. Acceptance: Finally believing and beginning to feel at peace.
We allow ourselves to calm down, rather than refueling the negative.

9. Healing: Getting our life back, no longer dwelling on issues.
We realize that everything takes us to different levels of our journey. Whatever happens will enrich the essence of our soul if we find the positive in it. Given time, we will be all right.

- - -

Regardless of any lesson each of us is required to learn, the one most important for all of us is unconditional forgiveness. When we forgive unconditionally, we allow ourselves to move beyond the pain, to start anew, and ultimately, inner peace.

- - - - -

Unconditional Forgiveness:
Attitudes are for looking out;
Principles are for looking in

As we are already aware, the first and most important step we can take to cope with a breach in any type of relationship which has led to heartbreak, is unconditional forgiveness. Not only do we allow ourselves a full release, enabling healing, a new beginning and ultimate wholeness, but we also diffuse the negativity surrounding the misdeed itself. We obtain the freedom to prepare ourselves for the more advanced lessons we have yet to encounter on our path.

Yet unconditional forgiveness can be difficult to attain, let alone practice, because it might initially be difficult to accept its meaning: As the name implies, we forgive unconditionally, without any conditions or expectations placed upon the party we are forgiving, including ourselves.

In its magnitude, this might seem unrealistic and impractical, yet its acceptance becomes easier when we realize that we are not we are not condoning the actions of any person or entity. Rather, we are reclaiming the power and freedom for ourselves that the actions, whether major or minor, have taken from us. We must now reclaim what was lost.

- - - - -

Begin to forgive others. . .

Unconditional forgiveness is a principle that applies for all people, on all levels. If someone has wronged us, we need to forgive them; if we have wronged another, we seek to be forgiven. What was done has passed, and it is now time to progress.

When we actively seek forgiveness from another, we may find that we cannot obtain it from them. Perhaps they are unable to forgive us because they have passed on, or maybe we have lost touch with them; perhaps they are accessible, but unwilling to forgive at this time.

Regardless of their availability or willingness, however, we are still worthy of forgiveness, be it either expressly from them, or from ourselves, should they be unable or otherwise unwilling to forgive us. We can allow ourselves this gift because we realize that, just as we seek to receive forgiveness, we are also capable of giving it to others, when necessary to do so.

. . .with self-forgiveness.

Forgiving ourselves is an important first step in forgiving others: in forgiving ourselves, we release the old issues and begin our own healing process, enabling us to face others with a clear mind and open heart.

For some of us, however, this may be the most difficult task we could ever hope to accomplish, depending upon our own unique set of experiences and situations. We may need to return to the past and reclaim the part of ourselves that has remained long-forgotten in the shadows, and in addition, review that incident which has caused us to seek self-forgiveness.

Each of us grew up believing the concepts, both about ourselves and the world around us, which our caregivers had relayed to us, either intentionally or perhaps even unintentionally. We might have been given a specific set of rules by which we were expected to behave; sometimes we were left alone to create them ourselves.

If we haven't reassessed these principles lately, we may find that the task is long overdue, for they reflect some else's consciousness and may no longer be appropriate to who we are now, or to whom we would like to become. If we have been treating ourselves (or others) with anything less than dignity and respect as a result of these principles, we need to discard them, for we have created a sense of separation as a result of their implementation. All of us are unified as One, since we were created from the same Source, and each of us is allowed the same Universal rights and privileges, regardless of our station in life. And, as we may have expected, one of these rights also includes the gift of forgiveness.

We then need to consider the nature of the offending action itself. If it is a minor one, one with an amicable solution that can be implemented and can repair any damage that had been caused, then we recognize the lesson, learn it as best we can, forgive ourselves (which we can easily do, regardless of whether the offended party has forgiven us or not), and get on with our lives.

But if we constantly replay the situation over and over in our minds, even long after the offended party had forgiven us and subsequently forgotten it, we need to release it now.

Many times, we tend to be too hard on ourselves, and in our exaggerated sense of conscience, we might become our own judge, jury and executioner. But in doing so, we only hurt ourselves and remain trapped in a false, counterproductive consciousness if it becomes second nature. When we know that, given the specific situation, we would probably forgive someone else had they committed the same offense, we need to allow ourselves the same latitude in forgiving ourselves as well.

But if the action was a major violation for which we cannot atone with the violated party or the family (even if we have tried), and we live daily with regret and shame resulting from our actions, we must remember that if we are still worthy of self-forgiveness. What has happened in the past cannot be changed, despite any present good intentions in the Now. If we truly regret our past actions and are now willing to atone for them, we can find other ways to repay the loss, even if reparation is not with the original party. But we must be serious enough to make that commitment, and we must have the awareness and patience to determine what we must do, and when it must be done.

We also remember that the offending action reflected where we were in our consciousness at that point in our lives, and according to chronological time. Sometimes the most important lessons that enable spiritual advancement are those that are most painful to learn.

In the Divine Order of things, Universal time shows us that past, present and future are as one: We are already forgiven, and we have learned our lessons. The only task remaining is that we must acknowledge this fact for ourselves.

- - - - -

In the Divine Order of things:
a Meditation to initiate self-forgiveness

As always, begin by breathing deeply, inhaling the positive and exhaling the negative. While you are breathing, find the White Light shining above you, warm, safe and comforting. Feel any pressures melting and falling away, while the White Light ever strengthens you, penetrating to your heart and illuminating your physical body. Feel this energy from the White Light.

When you are ready, turn and find the golden door. Open it, walk through it, up the flight of stairs and into the field beyond.

You are now in the peaceful place, the one where you are most comfortable, and where you attune with your Higher Self, finding all the answers you seek, true, good and from the Universe. As you again focus on the White Light which surrounds your body, you become one with it, melting into its white mist. Now, you begin to move forward with it.

All around you are other misty essences, and you realize that each is one such as yourself, for each has a physical body. And all of you recognize this: traveling together, you feel only love and warmth from the others around you, just as you feel the same for them.

Up in the distance is a bright Light which encompasses your entire view, One brighter than any you have ever seen. All of you move forward and merge with this Light; all are now One with it. Time and the past are One as well, for the only thing that matters is the peace you feel in the Now. You realize that you are here because, in the Divine Order of things, you are ready to release the past which has long held you back from your journey. Now, you are ready to move forward, for the price of your pain has yielded a greater wisdom than you could have ever known before.

- - - - -

When you are ready, slowly return to your present surroundings, carrying that Peace with you and throughout your day. You remember that all of us are as one with the Light, and as we move farther along our path, we are ready to open and commit ourselves to the greater and better.

Love, Trust and Forgiveness

There are times in our interpersonal relationships where our clear vision can become cloudy in the midst of our human emotions, especially when others might hurt or betray us in some manner.

If it is a close loved one who has committed the offense, the pain we feel surrounding the circumstances can be debilitating. If they attempt to steer us away from our own better judgment, their influence upon us can be critical, for those whom we love not only have the greatest capacity to hurt us the worst, but they can also influence us the most.

But when we choose to stay on the course of our own spiritual progression, our path might become less difficult to follow, our plans better formulated, and the resolutions easier to implement, when we move forward with the realization that unconditional love, trust and forgiveness are three separate, unrelated concepts.

As we are already aware, each of us, including our loved ones, are entitled to the Universal right of free will and choice, regardless of how we may have wanted them to handle the situation. And because each of us, as individuals, express ourselves differently, we cannot expect our loved ones to demonstrate their love for us in the same manner that we would show ours for them, nor can we necessarily trust them in the way we feel they should be trusted. Sometimes, our loved ones make mistakes, and even if their original intentions were well-meaning, we might be hurt nevertheless.

If our loved ones do somehow hurt or betray us, then, we realize that our spiritual progression continues unhindered when we separate the action of the human from the identity of the soul itself. Hence, when we forgive them unconditionally, we also allow ourselves the freedom for our own right action. And because we still love them unconditionally, we demonstrate to the Universe that we have learned the lessons involved in the situation: we do not have to trust them again once they have proven themselves untrustworthy.

- - - - -

129

As a Practical Matter:

There are two specific situations in which our interpersonal relationships might tempt us to stray off our own spiritual path and act in favor of our own human emotions. As we are already aware, the first was when we are hurt or betrayed by another. The other situation arises when another individual repeatedly expects our help to get out of a challenging situation (especially if we had helped once or twice before), when that situation is not ours to handle.

As we have already seen, when love and trust are not linked together in our interpersonal relationships, we can balance our own self-determination with right thought, tempered by forgiveness. For our own best course of action, we may need to reassess what expectations we had placed upon both the relationship itself, as well as those we had placed upon that individual.

Knowing that each of us has that free will and choice in our own responsibility for right action, we also allow others to do the same for themselves as well: we must remember that others should handle their own responsibilities alone. Any unwarranted infringement would deprive them of their lessons vital to their own spiritual growth.

If we are faced with either of these situations, what can we do, to determine the course of our own right action and mitigate our own emotional turmoil?

Before doing anything, we stop and think!

We need to impartially assess the situation and our options. Step back and visualize the situation from a Higher standpoint, rising above both the dispute and any anger or other inhibiting emotions. Not only do we see ourselves, but we also view the situation and other party involved in the dispute as well. We also remember to separate their actions from the identity of the soul (or who they are, versus what they have done).

We do not allow the actions stemming from the lower nature of the other individual influence us.

We remember that any actions they have committed are the result of their own perspective and consciousness at that time in their existence. If their actions were those based in malice and intent, we cannot allow ourselves to react from the same mindset. To do so would send out negative energy, which would only return to us in some manner at a later time.

For our own right action, we remember to plan according to the greatest good, for the greatest benefit for all. . .

Once we have cleared ourselves of any outside influences and any lower, ego-based mindsets, we meditate, and contemplate the most positive, constructive solutions and alternatives for the long-term benefit of all parties involved, even if the solution might be a painful one. Sometimes, the most valuable lessons are also those most difficult to learn. When we have decided upon the action, we commit ourselves, and do what needs to be done, and at the proper time.

If we have time to assess the situation, we ask our Higher Self for a resolution: We can write the question down, put it under our pillow, and sleep on it. When we are open, properly attuned, and receptive, we can try this for three consecutive days. The answer will come from the totality of mind-body-spirit perspective.

When we take our problems to our Higher source, we can tap into the collective Subconscious, or our Higher Self, the place where all the answers come. For many, answers manifest in the form of dreams, for it is in the sleep state when the conscious, everyday mind is at last stilled, allowing the most creative solutions to filter through the subconscious, and finally into the receptive part of the conscious mind.

And when we have accomplished these things. . .

We release the situation by giving it to the Universe.

Knowing that we cannot see the entire situation, we do our best to view the situation as objectively as we can, without passing judgment. Only the Universe can determine what events will allow each party the opportunity for the proper resolution; the situation is no longer ours to hold. We release the situation by giving it to the Universe, and then step back, allowing Them to handle it. Sometimes it is the most difficult thing we can do, but to enable a full release of the situation, however difficult as it might be, we must do so. In accomplishing this, we reclaim the power that we had lost when we placed it in a situation over which we had lost control.

The most important step to this process that we must wish only the best for others as we would for ourselves. As we might have expected, this means that we forgive then unconditionally; we remember that in the Divine Order of things, any energy sent out into the world will always return to the sender. This includes all energies, whether they be Love and Light, or malice and intent.

Similarly, if another individual chooses to send us negative energy, we do not accept it from them. We are allowed to send it back, without any repercussions against ourselves. All of us are from the One Source, and each of us is entitled to the Universal rights based in harmlessness. We would never wish negativity for others; hence, we would not wish it upon ourselves, either.

Similarly, the word, "hate" must always be avoided. A strong word that carries negative consequences, much pain and destruc-tion has resulted from its implementation and it is contrary to any type of spiritual advancement.

It cannot be stressed enough that all of us will get back the energy we send out into the world. Even though we may not directly witness that specific event manifesting the return of that energy, we may be assured nevertheless that such is the order of Natural law.

Hence, we must wish others well on their journey, and leave it for the Universe to handle, when we are unable to act rightly in our own self-protection.

- - - - -

It was the weekend again, but she didn't particularly care for weekends anymore. With all that the leisure time, they were alone together, faced with each other. But where else could she go?

Early Sunday morning, they had the usual discussion about

their differences: he taking the perspective that opposites balanced each other out; she feeling that she wanted to have a common spiritual bond together, but that it wasn't possible. They
were just too different.

It feels as though there's a fork in the road and you're going
one way, and I'm going the other, she said. How often had she
repeated that, in so many words?

How about if I go with you? he asked, seemingly hopeful.

No, she replied. Though he did not yet seem to know his
path, hers somehow didn't fit him. He'd shown no interest in
hers until now.

You need to go where your spirit goes, was all she said. She
surprised herself when a tear slipped out of the far corner of her
right eye.

How could she be so emotional about something she felt was
so right?

He proffered, Even though we're on different paths, we could
still hold hands if our arms are long enough...

She laughed. What a beautiful thought! And it was, too.

But it was also heart-wrenching. Was she supposed to stay?

She became silent, unsure. But the silence only magnified
her uncertainty.

Who is to say what is right or wrong?

The changes began two years ago, when you seemed to head
off in your own direction, she said. I'd seen it earlier that year:
you were restless, anxious. I couldn't understand why. Then, we
went out West; a part of you seemed driven to commune alone in
the mountains. You were going, listening to something neither of
us could hear. I couldn't keep up with you! Seeing that, I began
to let go then...

When we do what we need to do, the people in our lives in
some way affect it. Depending upon whatever it is we need to
do, and what they need to do—sometimes they end up falling
away.

Can you understand that? That was the question she never
asked aloud.

He could see that things weren't working anymore. He had
at least admitted that his entire life had been one of pain; with
the dissonance between them, he was frightened of the inevitable

pain he would have to feel after a breakup. And so he was willing to stay long after the last ember had died and there was nothing left but the cold, grey ashes.

But she knew that the pain was unavoidable for them both, whether or not they stayed together. For just as she was beginning to find her path and her strength, pieces of him were falling away. His usual activities seemed to leave him empty nowadays. And as the time passed, his confusion was draining his strength.

Fool! yelled the voice inside of her head. He has always been kind and faithful. The only issue is that we're moving in opposite directions. Do people really break up solely for that reason? Maybe I am the problem.

The argument had a hollow ring. She knew she was right, but she felt guilty, selfish. Maybe I should just shut up and get along. I don't want to hurt him.

Nowadays, things were changing for the better: They had finally resolved the issues they'd fought over when they were first married. There was now nothing wrong with the marriage. They were friends at last.

But I believe that when good people do good things, that good returns to them. Isn't that the Universal law? The Universe rewards right action. He's been putting out good energy for me, but it's not returning to him—I cannot give him what he seeks. And so he is hurting. If I hurt him, I must be bad. But I don't think I'm bad. How can I give him something that I am incapable of giving?

What's wrong with me? The question haunted her.

- - - - -

Later that same afternoon, they took a short drive to visit some friends who were planning a trip further out West than in the years past. Did they want to go, too? Nobody wanted to do the annual trip anymore.

Neither knew how to respond.

Let us know what you think, so we can make reservations for you both, their friend said, looking at each of them separately.

As they drove home, he asked her, smiling as though nothing were wrong, Do you want to go?

Not really, she responded casually. There was nothing left to say.

But she loved the thought of traveling again. She could see the green treeline in the distance, the craggy brown mountains. They were calling to her. But she couldn't go and act as though everything was fine. It just wasn't working anymore.

Only happy couples go to pretty places and have a good time, she thought sarcastically.

But everything seems fine, she thought stubbornly. Maybe there is nothing wrong. Maybe I should just get along. . .

Pulling into the garage, he noticed that the lights were off. Hey! The power's out! Not again! he muttered, disgusted.

She wasn't surprised. In this heat, she figured it would be only matter of time before a transformer blew in the neighborhood—she was surprised that the electricity had lasted this long. In their fourteen years here, this was the third power outage—the first two happened in the previous two years.

Sure enough, the power was out, and half the neighborhood was down, too.

She suddenly realized that when she first became aware that something was wrong with their marriage, there was a power outage!

Both of the other times the power had been out, he had been out of town, fishing. She had sat alone and contemplated silence in the house; without the whir and hum of the appliances, the walls seemed to come alive, as if they were resonating the energy they had absorbed over the years. Everything had become sharper, clearer. The place was alive with their differences.

Now, it was as if the Universe was telling her to pay attention! A vacation now would only be a distraction from the real issues. If she went, everything would still be just as wrong as it had been before.

Sitting in the fading light, she realized that they had to do what they needed to do, each for themselves. Though all she felt was sadness that her path was not where his would go, she knew that they both would be all right, despite the sadness now. Given time, each would find their own way. She realized that he knew more than what he was allowing himself to feel, to know; left alone to face himself, he would find it.

What more could either ask?

- - - - -

Finally:

We must always remember:

We have everything we need right now,
to live the life we are dreaming of;

The more we love ourselves and enjoy this life,
the more we honor the One Who created us;

The more we manifest our true beauty
and express our unique gift,
the more the Universe will rejoice.

- - - - -

Epilogue

Being able to step away from the emotional side of ourselves is very difficult, for we are, after all, only human. Though we tend to be controlled by our own ever-present fears, inadequacies and indecisiveness, we must use them as tools, or they will use us.

Experts will always tell us in that ridding ourselves of old habits, needless anxieties and frivolous thoughts, we will allow ourselves to become who we truly are–at peace, balanced within ourselves, confident and ready each day, to embrace our life more than ever before.

What we can hope for, then, is a new beginning, attracting people and situations better suited to us as we learn and grow after each change, challenge, and finally, conclusion in all things. We must ever evolve, change and grow—we must not draw back! We need to embrace our lives and heal ourselves. Isn't that what our lessons were in days of old?

Many of us assume that life should always be peaceful. My belief, however, is that in everything we can attain peace with our choices and the decisions we make.

What we can do is stop reacting negatively. If we expect little, that what's attracted. Step back, smile, learn to appreciate the gifts we were given, and know that we are alone only to contemplate. Rising above our innermost fears can be done, keeping in mind that there is a greater plan, a bigger picture for all of us. Inner peace can be attained–it isn't elusive! We must never assume that life comes without crisis; the Universal plan isn't always ours to know. Whatever our situation, it's forever changing, evolving and taking experience, memories and hope with us. After all, this too, shall pass. At the end of the day, things and events can come together again.

Don't be afraid! When we feel as if we are walking a tightrope, wondering if there is a right way to handle ourselves, we must put one foot in front of the other to begin our Journey again. We must listen to those first thoughts and quiet the chatter.

We are all special and the Light will always prevail. It doesn't matter how hard or arduous the path is. What we take from each and every experience, how we implement that power–this is where the focus should be, and can be.

Step into the future -
by now we know the way

Gone are all our fears
the hangups of yesterday.

Know yourself, free yourself
break all the ties that bind

Not just your heart,
not just your soul
no confines of your mind.

Reach out for all that
awaits
and know your life is always your own.

Like a song on the wind,
what we hear first
is always
the pitch,
then the tone. . .

Joy Mills, C.Ht. is an internationally known clairvoyant. Born in St. Louis, Missouri, she resided in several Southeastern states before she and her family returned to Missouri.

Following the discovery of her clairvoyant abilities at age three, she endured the skepticism and abuse of various family members, but through the encouragement and support of her grandmother, Joy came to accept her birthright and realize that she was meant to use it by assisting those who needed, and sought her help.

There were two significant events which permanently altered the course of Joy's life, and ultimately led her to using her gifts on a full-time basis. In 1984, Joy suffered a near-fatal, debilitating automobile accident, followed by a long and arduous path to near-complete recovery. Six years later, in a separate incident, she was pronounced clinically dead. It was during the aftermath of this most profound time that Joy found herself standing at a crossroads: She began to fully realize not only her clairvoyant abilities, but the significance of her own spirituality and the ultimate meaning it would hold for her as well. She reconsidered her career with a greater perspective and appreciation, and began her life again with a full acceptance of her true birthright and destiny, this time using her gifts for the greatest benefit of all–helping others.

Today, Joy's activities are many and varied. They include author, teacher, and lecturer. In her private practice, her clients reside not only in the U.S., but Canada, the United Kingdom, Japan, China, Russia, South America and Australia as well. She conducts workshops and has appeared on radio, national and international television. Presently, Joy is negotiating a syndicated newspaper column. Joy has also worked to locate missing persons, and in certain cases, her time and efforts are donated.

For more information about Joy's other publications or audio tapes, write to:

Lightsource Publications
Attn: Joy Mills and Associates LLC
P.O. Box 2224
St. Peters, MO 63376